# CLEOPATRA

*Adèle Geras*
Illustrated by M P Robertson

KINGFISHER

THIS ONE IS FOR
GUY HENRY JONES
A.G.

THANKS TO JENNY (CLEO)
AND ELLIE (NEFRET)
M.P.R.

KINGFISHER

Kingfisher Publications Plc
New Penderel House
283–288 High Holborn
London WC1V 7HZ
www.kingfisherpub.com

First published by Kingfisher Plc 2007
10 9 8 7 6 5 4 3 2 1
ITR/0607/LFG/SCHOY(SCHOY)/157MA/C



Publisher: Melissa Fairley
Senior Designer: Jane Tassie
Senior Editor: Alison Stanley
Consultant: Dr Thorsten Opper, Department of Greek and Roman Antiquities, The British Museum
Production Manager: Nancy Roberts
DTP Co-ordinator: Catherine Hibbert
Indexer: Polly Goodman

A CIP catalogue record for this book is available from the British Library.

ISBN 978 0 7534 1359 3

Printed in China

# Contents

# Nefret's Diary

Nefret's diary entries tell of events that happened between the years we now call 41–40BCE. She also refers to historical events – such as the civil war between Roman generals Julius Caesar and Pompey – that happened as far back as 49BCE. Nefret could not have known these dates, so they are not used in her diary extracts. Like most ordinary people in Egypt, Nefret did not use a calendar or give names to the months. A calendar was used for official business, by scientists and scribes and other important people.

# Before Sunset

## Third month. Five days before the full moon.

My name is Nefret, which means 'pretty'. My mother says I'm lucky, too. That's because I can read and write. My friend, Rami, who is the son of one of the palace scribes, taught me everything he learned. This means I can set down all the important things that happen to me. Rami has given me some papyrus scrolls to use as a diary and I shall start writing now, because I have much to tell. At the next full moon, when I'm ten, I shall be going to work for Queen Cleopatra at the royal palace. I can't wait to live in the palace! Both my brothers have grown up and left home, but my little sister, Kebi, shares a sleeping mat with me. She kicks me in the night. It will be lovely to have a mat all to myself.

Women in our family have always worked for the royal household. I hope that when the time comes for me to leave my mother's house, Lotus Blossom, my beautiful, green-eyed cat, can come with me. She sits beside me as I write, and looks down at the papyrus as if she's reading a story.

I live in Egypt: in Alexandria, a port that's always crowded with ships from all over the Mediterranean Sea. The royal family's house is here too. It's a splendid palace guarded by soldiers. Behind the palace are the small houses where the servants of the royal household, including my parents and Rami's parents, live.

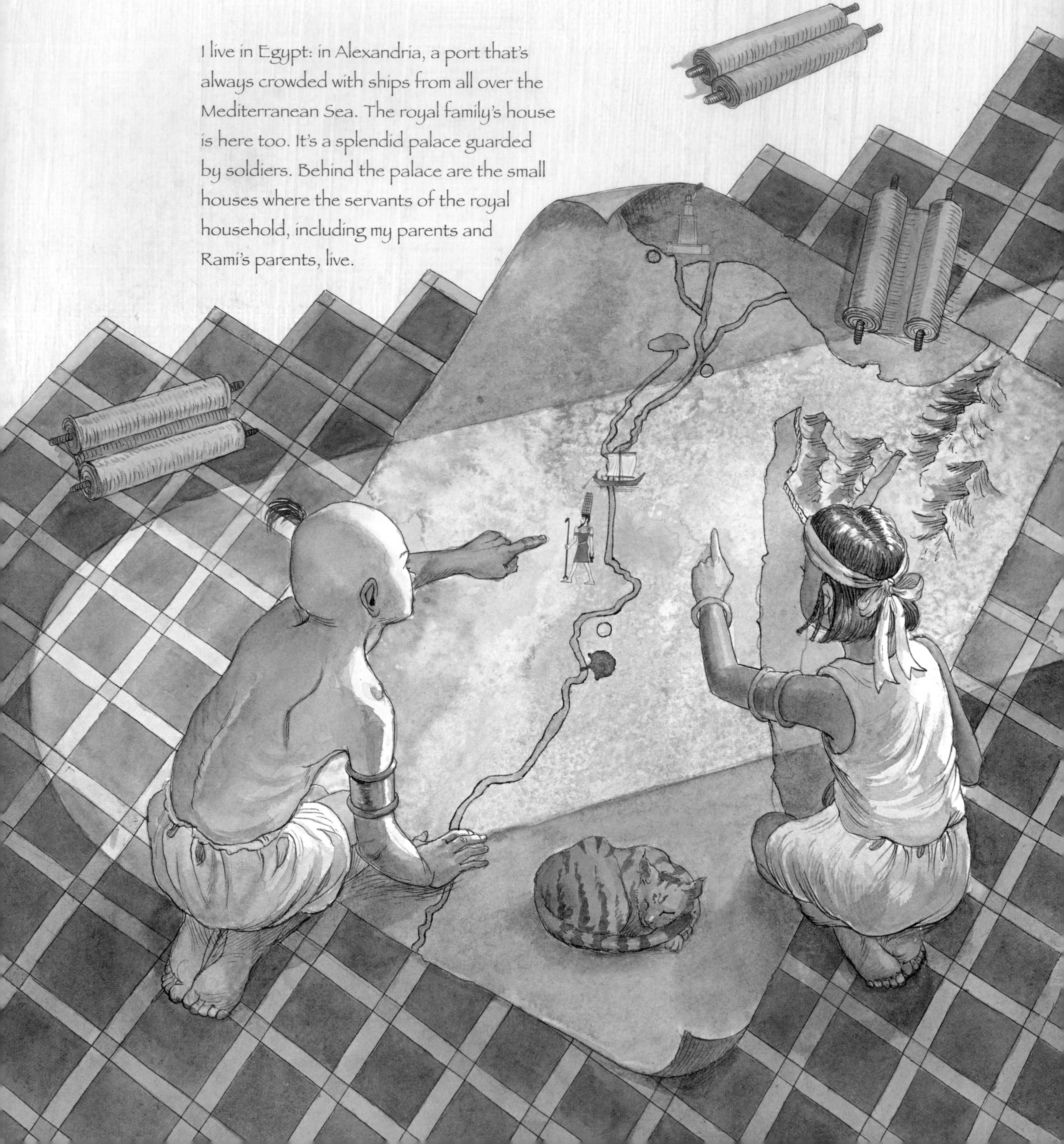

Rami isn't my only friend. I have many companions. My best girlfriends are Nanu and Sheriti. They help me look after Kebi sometimes. We play games and go swimming and take part in gymnastic competitions. Kebi likes those best, because she's better at running and jumping than I am. But I'm a stronger swimmer and Kebi doesn't even know how to write her name! I hope some of my friends will come to work in the palace when I do, or who will I play with when my work is done?

Our river, the Nile, floods the surrounding plains once a year and then there's enough wheat and barley to feed all the people. In the temples devoted to our gods, we offer prayers that the river may continue to give us all the food we need. In years when the floods don't come, then the people starve and there's almost no grain in the huge grain stores.

Lotus miaows very loudly when she's hungry, but there always seem to be mice around for her to catch, so she'll be all right. I just hope there's enough food in the palace for me!

*When the River Nile floods, there is a good harvest and plenty of grain for everyone.*

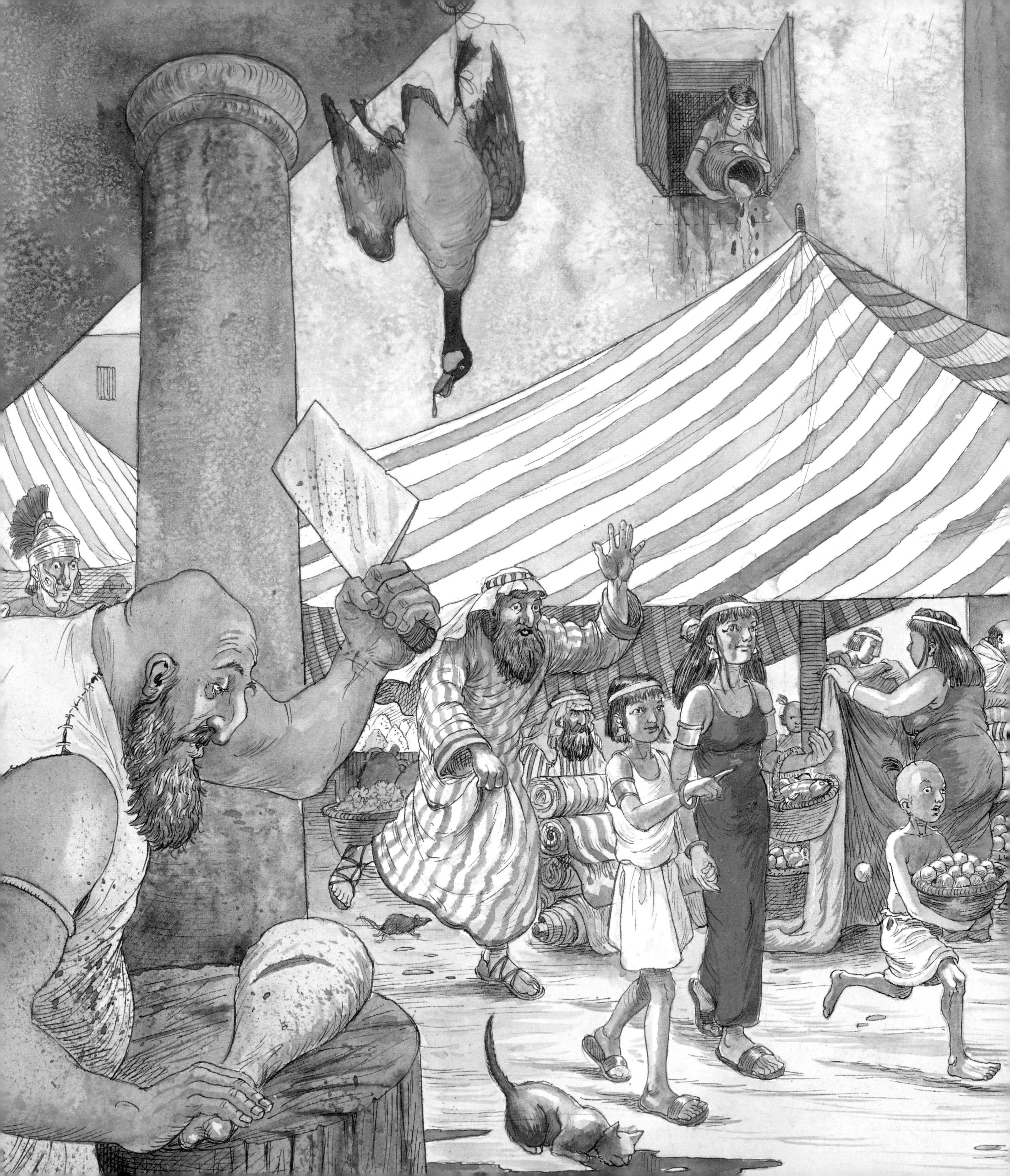

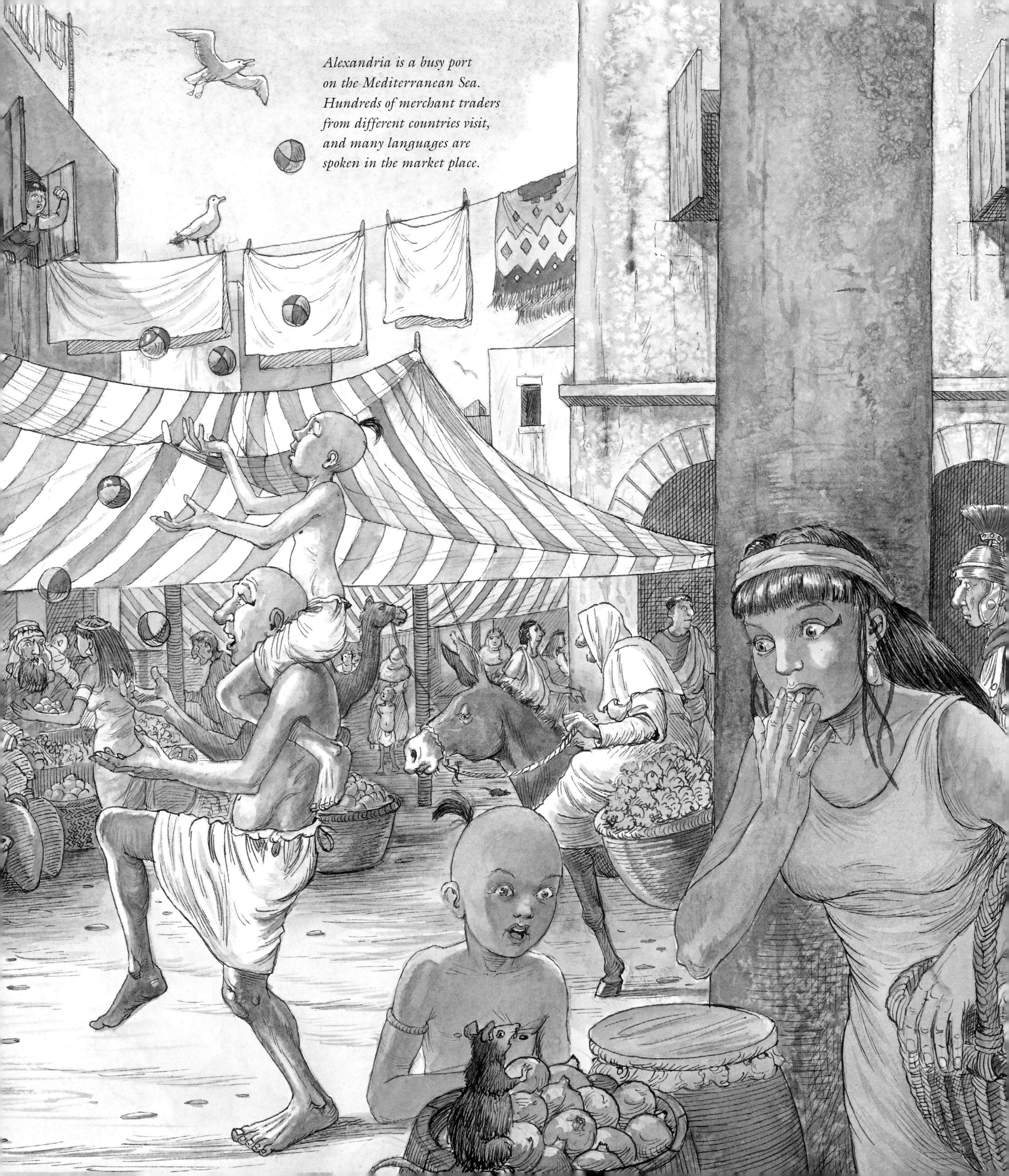

*Alexandria is a busy port on the Mediterranean Sea. Hundreds of merchant traders from different countries visit, and many languages are spoken in the market place.*

My mother has told me many things about Queen Cleopatra. I have decided to write them all down in this diary, before I go and work at the palace. Then, when I meet the queen, she will be amazed that I already seem to know her!

I know that the queen is not exactly beautiful, but so charming that everyone who meets her thinks she is the loveliest person they've ever seen. Her smile is enchanting and so is her voice. She's very clever and can speak nine languages. I can only speak Egyptian and a little bit of Cat, which is useful for when I'm talking to Lotus.

Here's what else I know. The queen's family was from Macedonia, but she was born in Egypt and wants to make us as powerful as the Romans. My mother says she had a great struggle to become our queen, overcoming many enemies to do so. She was only seventeen when she came to the throne. She wasn't allowed to rule on her own, but had to have a husband, so she married one of her younger brothers, Ptolemy. My mother said it was a marriage in name only, which means she didn't have to kiss her brother or anything like that. If I had to marry one of my brothers, I'd run away for ever!

*The queen's brother-husband, Ptolemy, had some scheming advisors who plotted against Cleopatra.*

Ptolemy was much younger than Cleopatra, so she was the real ruler. But Ptolemy didn't like the idea of not being a ruler. He didn't like being bossed about by his sister and he had some scheming men to advise him. These advisors of Ptolemy's were quite old men and they hated Cleopatra being the queen. They were always plotting against her.

Cleopatra had trouble with the Romans as well. The Roman empire was enormous and because there were so many men in the Roman legions, feeding and paying them all was a problem. The Romans were always trying to get hold of Egypt's grain and jewels and gold. Two important Roman generals were fighting one another. They were called Julius Caesar and Pompey. Julius Caesar won a big sea battle at Pharsalus, so Pompey fled to Alexandria, thinking that young Ptolemy would protect him.

*Julius Caesar*

*Pompey*

I must stop writing now. It's time for my dancing lesson. I love dancing and this is my best lesson of all. I will see Nanu and Sheriti, but first I must find the dress I have to wear. Perhaps Kebi's hidden it? She does this sometimes and then I get so annoyed that I say I'll pull her hair. She hates having her hair pulled, so she always tells me where it is at once.

# Just After Dawn

## THIRD MONTH. FOUR DAYS BEFORE THE FULL MOON.

I am writing this before the morning meal. Lotus woke me by jumping on my pillow and leaving a few feathers there. Ugh! She's been chasing birds… they're her favourite early-morning snack. Now I can't get back to sleep. My mother didn't want to tell me about the death of the Roman general, Pompey, because she thought it might give me nightmares. But I asked Rami and he told me what happened. He knows a lot of things. Our families have arranged for us to be married, but that's not for ages yet, when I'm almost thirteen. I won't mind marrying him. He's always nice to me.

Rami told me that horrible young Ptolemy gave orders to his men to kill Pompey. Ptolemy wanted to please Julius Caesar. He thought Caesar would like to see the head of his enemy brought to him in a straw basket. He was wrong. Caesar was furious, and also very sad, because Pompey used to be one of his allies. Julius Caesar ordered Ptolemy and Cleopatra to come and see him.

*Julius Caesar was horrified when he realised what Ptolemy had done.*

*Cleopatra arranged for her trusted bodyguard to deliver a very special carpet to the palace.*

My mother told me what happened next. She said that Cleopatra wanted to see Julius Caesar without Ptolemy, so that she could tell him that her little brother was not to be trusted. She arranged for a boat to be rowed to the palace jetty and in that boat was a rolled-up carpet. The oarsman shouted up to the guards: 'Hey, there's a delivery here for Julius Caesar. One very beautiful oriental carpet. It's urgent.'

No one asked why the carpet had to be delivered so urgently. They probably thought that if Caesar had ordered it, he'd want it brought to him at once. So they opened the gate and the man in the boat lifted the rolled-up carpet on to his shoulder. When he reached the room Caesar was in, he lowered the carpet to the floor and let it unroll across the marble floor.

'And guess what happened next?' my mother said when she told me the story. I couldn't guess. When she told me, I laughed so much that Lotus jumped off my lap and went to hide behind a screen.

*Cleopatra had to be smuggled into Caesar's room because she did not trust Ptolemy or his advisors.*

Cleopatra had been rolled up in the carpet all the time! As soon as it was unrolled, she jumped out and smiled at Julius Caesar. And when he saw her, he fell in love with her. My mother says Cleopatra has a magic about her which makes every man who sees her love her.

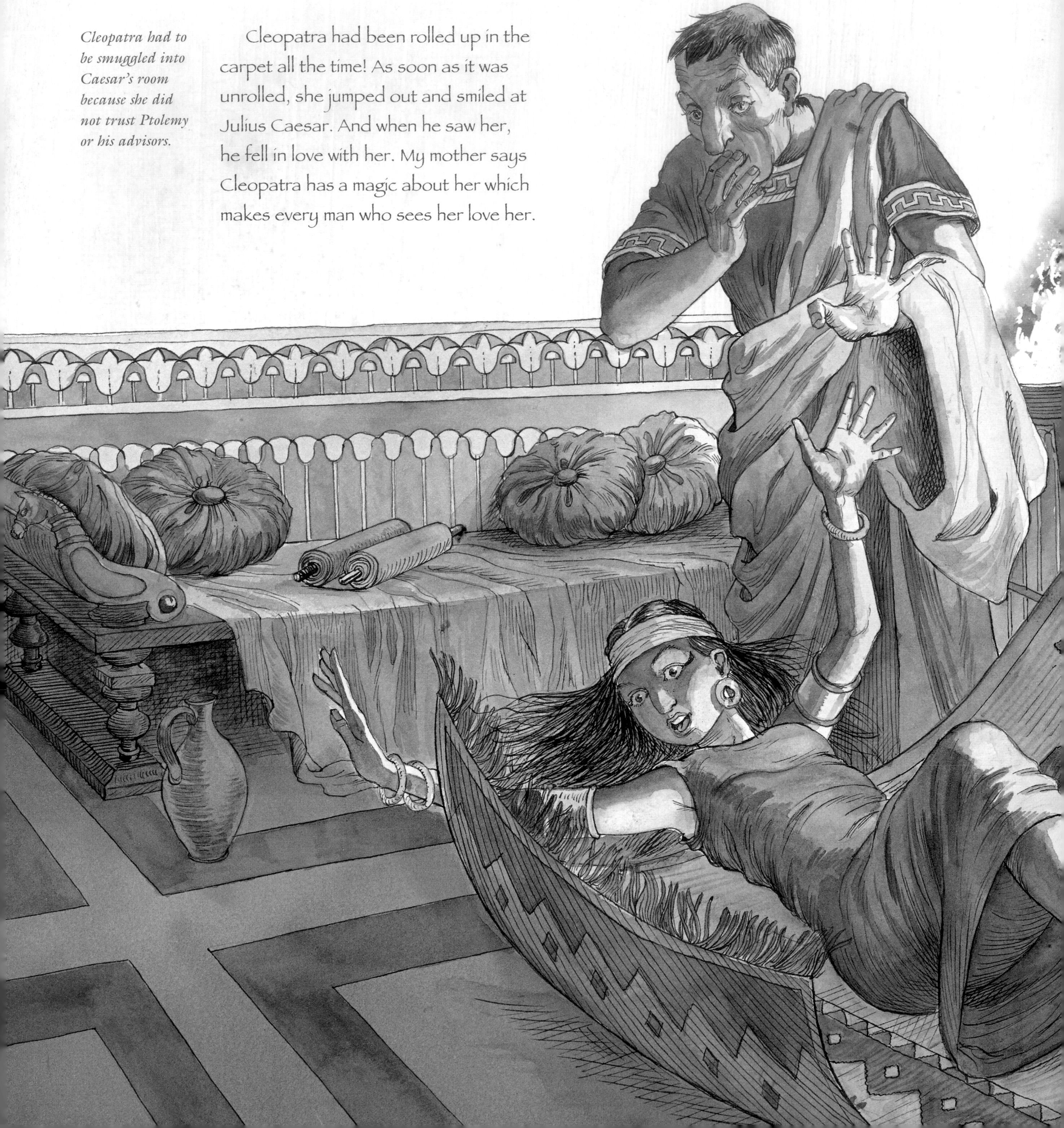

Now it's time to clear away my writing material for today. My mother has gone to prepare the morning meal. Lotus knows that there will be milk for her and I can smell the bread baking.

# *Before Sunset*

## THIRD MONTH. TWO DAYS BEFORE THE FULL MOON.

Rami has just shown me how to write the queen's name in the picture writing that the scribes use. I feel very clever! I copied what he showed me so well that he praised me for my skill.

When Rami left, I went to find my mother. I asked her to finish telling me about Cleopatra and Julius Caesar, because the day after my birthday I'm moving to the palace. Sometimes I feel excited about this, but I'm also a little nervous. The queen's husband was found drowned in the Nile. Did she and Caesar plot to get rid of him? If the queen can have her own brother killed, what might she do to a maidservant?

*Cleopatra's name as a 'cartouche', written in Egyptian hieroglyphics by Rami.*

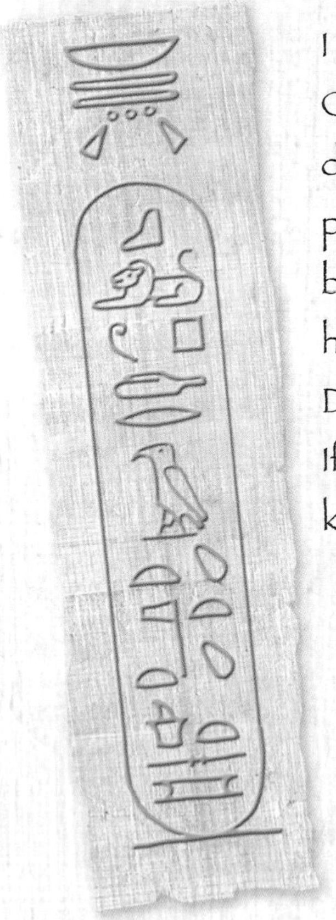

My mother told me that everyone knew Julius Caesar and Queen Cleopatra were in love. But it wasn't just love that made them take a long trip down the River Nile. They wanted to be seen by the Egyptian people together – the queen of Egypt and one of the rulers of Rome. I was much younger then, but I do remember my mother taking me to the port to see them go.

'Nefret,' my mother said, 'the royal barge had never looked as fine as this before. It was specially decorated for the voyage. The cabins were filled with servants and food and wine. Musicians played beautiful music, while Cleopatra and Caesar lay about on cushions. They wanted to show everyone in the country how powerful the queen was, and how friendly she was with the most powerful man in Rome.'

I thought it sounded like a kind of holiday, and I pictured them spending hours staring into one another's eyes, curled up together, just like me and Lotus. I'd love to go sailing down the river but Lotus would hate it. She does not like getting her fur wet!

I listened intently as my mother continued. 'On Cleopatra and Julius Caesar's trip, the river was in flood and

Egyptians believe that as queen, Cleopatra is the goddess Isis come down to Earth.

all you could see in some places was water from the ship to the horizon.' My mother said that when they reached the temple of the goddess Isis in Philae, they sailed between the columns by candlelight.

Everyone knows that the queen is the goddess, come down to Earth. They say she sometimes puts on clothes like the ones the goddess wears in the many pictures of her that decorate the walls of the palace. These garments are made of gold. She wears a feather cape around her shoulders, and every feather is painted with liquid gold leaf.

*Cleopatra's ten-year-old brother-husband liked having the protection of the Roman soldiers.*

'A short while after their trip,' my mother continued, 'Julius Caesar went back to Rome. But he left three legions of Roman soldiers behind to protect Cleopatra... and to protect Rome's interest in Egypt. Cleopatra still had to have a husband, so she married her other little brother, Ptolemy, and he was only ten years old!'

While Caesar was away, the queen gave birth to Caesar's son, Ptolemy-Caesar, known as Caesarion. She thought that their child would be able to reign over Egypt and also rule the Roman empire when he grew up.

Cleopatra missed Julius Caesar so much, that she followed him to Rome. She stayed there for two years and Caesar gave her money and treasures of all kinds. She lived in great splendour and there was even a statue dedicated to her in the Temple of Venus.

*Julius Caesar was murdered on a day people called the 'Ides of March'.*

But not everyone was happy. The Romans didn't think their leader should be so friendly with an Egyptian queen. They didn't want Caesar thinking he was a king. They were worried, too, that the power of the Roman empire might pass to an Egyptian.

Then, a terrible thing happened. On the fourteenth day of the third month, Caesar was brutally stabbed to death by his enemies.

My mother said that Queen Cleopatra was so frightened of what might happen without Caesar to protect her, she decided to come home to Egypt.

So that's why she needs more servants to work for her, and one of them is to be me! I wonder if I'll have to look after her little boy? I don't think I'd like to very much. I remember Kebi when she was two. She used to cry a lot and sometimes smelled. Cats are much cleaner and they always sleep well.

# Sunset

## Third month. Full moon.

*Music and dancing are an important part of every celebration. Girls usually dance in pairs – and never with boys – and dances include acrobatics.*

We've been celebrating my tenth birthday. My mother made so much food! And all my relatives came to visit us and join in the feast. It was good to see my brothers again. All my friends have given me gifts: carved wooden animals and charms to hang on the necklace my parents gave me. The dancing master arranged a dance in my honour and all my friends took part in the display. It has been a wonderful time.

Tomorrow morning, I will go with my mother to the palace. I must take my papyrus scrolls with me, but I don't know if I will find time to write about my life in the palace. Lotus is coming with me because the queen loves cats! I hope there are still lots of soldiers to protect the queen at the palace. Lotus isn't a very good guard cat. She'd be very scared if anyone came banging on the doors.

# Early Morning

## FIFTH MONTH. THREE-QUARTER MOON.

I've been living at the palace for nearly two months. There has been too much to learn and I haven't been able to find a quiet time to write 'til now.

When I first arrived at the palace, I thought the queen would be too unhappy to talk to me. She must have been so sad, still, about Julius Caesar. Then her other brother-husband died and people were saying he'd been poisoned. But she was really kind to me.

'Nefret,' she said, 'you are worthy of your name. Welcome to my palace. And you have a cat, I'm told, who's coming to live here too. What's her name?'

'Lotus Blossom, my lady. I call her Lotus.'

'She's welcome too. My beloved Topaz will be happy to have a friend. He was lonely while we were away in Rome.'

As soon as I heard Cleopatra speak, I knew I'd do anything she asked of me. Her voice was like the sweetest music and I felt happy when I listened to it.

My duties are to attend the queen at ceremonial occasions and I have the care of her night garments. I have to see that they are taken to the washerwomen and returned to the chest where I strew them with fragrant herbs. Sometimes, I'm in the chamber when the queen is dressed.

I have never seen such fine clothes as Cleopatra has in her sandalwood chests. There is fine-spun wool dyed in rich colours. There is linen, too, and everything is decorated by the fine stitching of the palace embroiderers, who sew pretty pictures and patterns around the hems and sleeves of every dress.

*Cleopatra's favourite bracelet is in the form of a gold snake that winds up her arm.*

Her golden Isis costume has a chest of its own. Every headdress Cleopatra wears is put away in a box when she has finished wearing it. Each one is studded with gemstones the size of small onions and sewn with gold and silver coins that glitter as the queen passes by. On all the gold coins used to buy and sell things in Egypt, she is dressed as Isis, and her son, Caesarion, is shown as the god Horus.

She has got carved wooden chests overflowing with necklaces, brooches, jewel-encrusted headbands and bracelets. Coral from the ocean bed makes her necklaces; moonstones from the desert glow in her rings. Her bed is decorated with paintings of waterlilies and cats and hawks. The snake, sacred to Isis, is her favourite creature and she has a gold bracelet in the form of an asp that winds all the way up her arm.

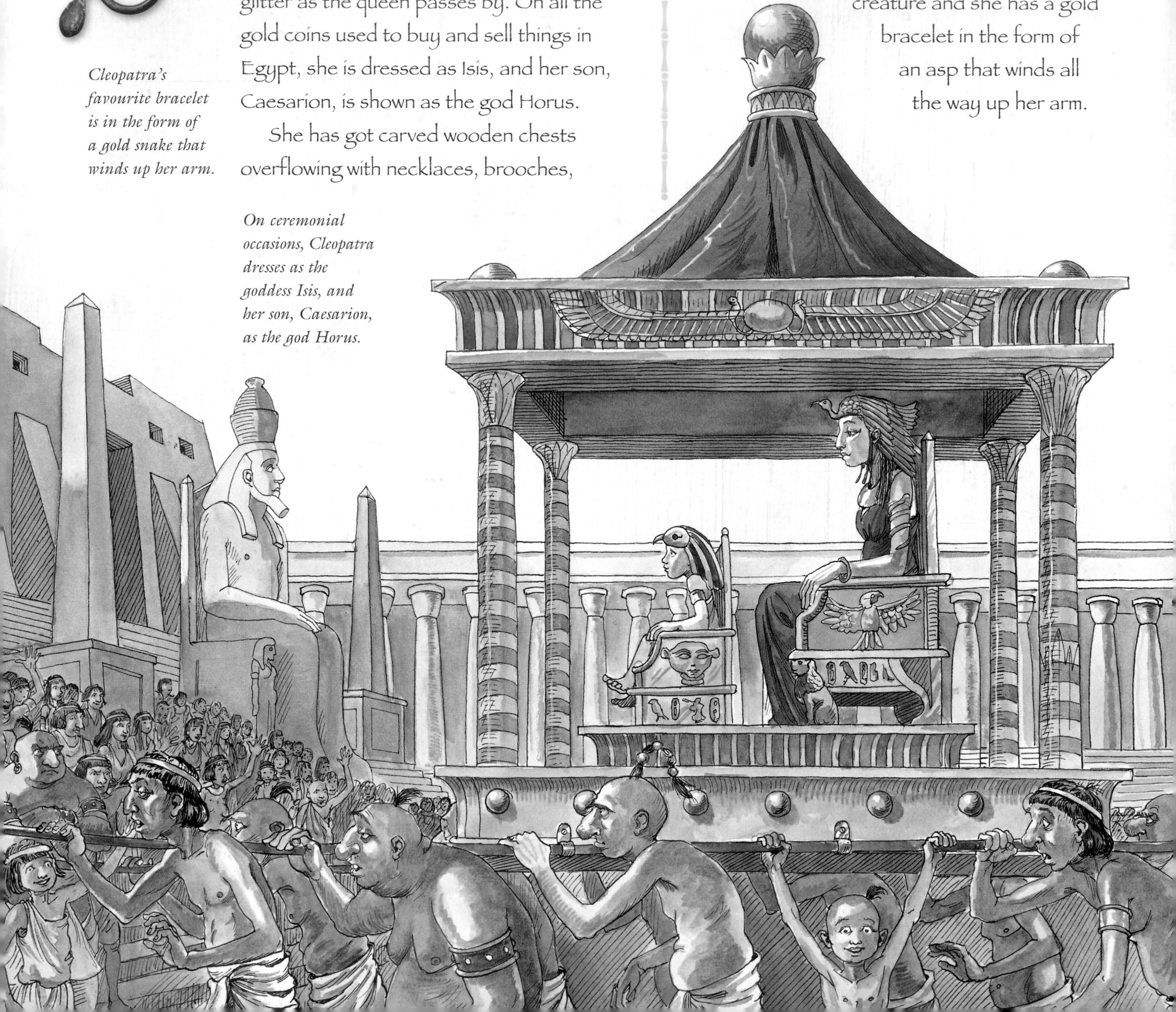

*On ceremonial occasions, Cleopatra dresses as the goddess Isis, and her son, Caesarion, as the god Horus.*

As well as being careful always to appear in her finest robes and precious stones, Cleopatra also reads a lot and studies many things.

The queen spends much of her time in the library, learning about the world and all the marvels that may be found in it. She reads scrolls about science, astrology and history. She also knows how to calculate with numbers and how to decipher codes and strange languages. I'd love to be as clever as that.

*Cleopatra is well known for her intelligence. She reads a great deal and can speak nine languages.*

# Afternoon

## Seventh month. Two days before the full moon.

Last night, I was too nervous to sleep. I, Nefret, had been chosen by the queen to be a handmaiden on a journey she was making to Tarsus. She was going to the camp of Marc Antony, one of the rulers of the Roman empire. I'd been told that he wanted to make sure that Cleopatra had not ganged up against him by making an alliance with his enemies.

'Nefret,' the queen said to me, 'you must come with me on this voyage. You're my prettiest handmaiden. Everyone on the banks will stare at us as we pass and when Marc Antony sees my barge in all its splendour, he'll be dazzled by the sight, I promise you.'

*The royal barge is loaded with food and drink for the journey to Tarsus.*

# Early Morning

## Seventh month. Full moon.

The day before we set sail was so busy. All the cooks and serving-women made many trips to and from the kitchens, bringing all the food and drink that we were going to need on to the royal barge. I was feeling nervous before we set off. Waving goodbye to my mother and Kebi made me wish they were coming too. Lotus wasn't there to say goodbye, but I knew she would miss me and I would long for her company as well. But the barge was so splendid!

The sails of our vessel were cut from purple silk and three men had worked for days painting the high stern with fresh gold leaf. I was one of six handmaidens and we were dressed as mermaids in sea-green jewelled robes.

Our hair had been plaited with silver threads. My dress fitted me as tightly as another skin, and as the sun shone on us during the journey, I grew more and more uncomfortable. But I held myself very straight and remembered to smile, as the queen herself had instructed. Musicians played their flutes as we sailed up the river. The melodies floated over the water, and the sailors bent their oars to the rhythm.

Cleopatra, dressed up as Aphrodite, was wearing a robe made of such delicate fabric that her perfect figure could be seen through the embroidered cloth. She lay on a couch heaped with silken pillows and young boys dressed as cupids fanned her with enormous peacock-feather fans.

*Men have worked for days getting the ship ready for the journey.*

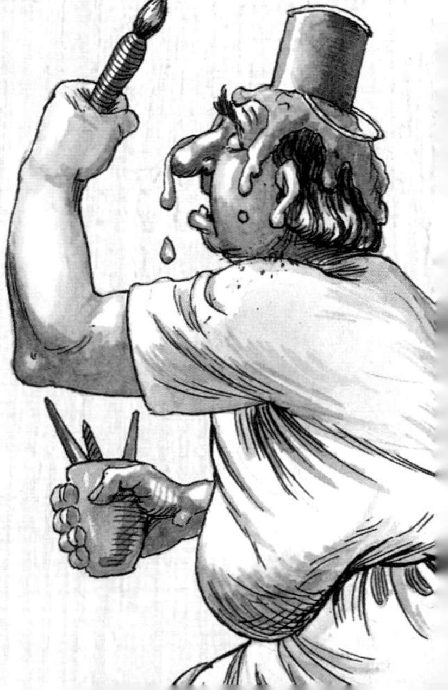

Many people had gathered on the bank to stare at the queen as our ship sailed towards Tarsus, but there was no sign of Marc Antony. Cleopatra was determined that he would come to her. She was a queen and also a goddess. She wasn't going to leave her ship to go and see him, even if he was one of the most powerful men in Rome. She had wanted him to come to Egypt to see her, but he wouldn't. So she decided that the ship she was on was a part of her kingdom, because she was on it. The ship, she said, is Egypt, so that's where he had to come! People don't like to cross the queen when she's in this mood. They also remember what happened to her brothers.

In the end, Marc Antony came down to the water's edge and then on to the barge to dine with Cleopatra. I wonder whether he's going to fall in love with her, just like Julius Caesar did?

# Early Morning

## SEVENTH MONTH. THIRD DAY AFTER THE FULL MOON.

*Many people think Cleopatra is too extravagant. But the Romans love good food, and Cleopatra needs them on her side.*

I had never seen such a banquet! Thousands of rush-lights flickered in every part of the ship and were reflected in the black waters of the river. The palace cooks were famous and Marc Antony ate and drank as he had never eaten and drunk before. I heard him say so, for I was near him, trying to stop the naughty boys who were dressed as cupids from helping themselves to the food. There were stuffed, roasted boars, peacocks which had been cooked and then decorated with their own gorgeous tail feathers spread out, mountains of fruit glazed with sugar and cakes soaked in honey.

At the end of this meal, Cleopatra took one of her pearl earrings and dropped it into her goblet. Then she drank the wine down quickly, and Marc Antony's eyes opened wide to see such extravagance: imagine thinking so little of a precious pearl that you can swallow it! It was obvious that our queen had impressed him. She must be wealthy beyond his wildest dreams, and also as bewitching as everyone said she was. He couldn't stop looking at her. When Marc Antony and Cleopatra had finished eating, I was dismissed, together with all the other servants. Cleopatra was alone with him at last.

I went to where the mats were laid out for the handmaidens. I was the youngest and the others were very nice to me. When I lay down, I thought of Lotus going to sleep on some other mat in the palace. Maybe she'd been having her own little banquet of mice.

*Cleopatra is determined to win Marc Antony's heart, in order to protect Egypt. She is using all her powers to woo him.*

# Very Early Morning

## Eighth month. Waning moon.

We are still at Tarsus. I'm beginning to wonder when we are to return to Alexandria as I am missing my family and Lotus.

Marc Antony invited the queen to a banquet in his camp and this time she accepted. The older handmaidens said Marc Antony was determined to give Queen Cleopatra an even better feast than the one she had organised for him. All the queen's handmaidens attended her, but we did not have to wear our mermaid robes. I'm glad, because mine was so tight and hot.

Marc Antony was really loud and vulgar all evening. He told lots of rude jokes but the queen laughed at them – she must really like him! Everyone was lying down to eat. They rested on one elbow and used the other arm to reach for their food and drink. They even fed each other, by dangling things like grapes over each other's mouths. My mother would not be happy to see this. She makes us sit down on the floor, crossed legs, and eat with both hands. But some of the food did look delicious – though nothing could be as wonderful as the banquet we had on the royal barge.

We didn't get back to the boat until almost sunrise! I could hardly keep my eyes open, but when we got back I still had to help with the queen's clothing. Tomorrow we are to return to Alexandria. I'm longing to see my mother and sister, and all my friends, especially Rami. They might even be a little envious of me. I hope Lotus remembers me.

*Marc Antony wants to show Cleopatra that the Romans can entertain too.*

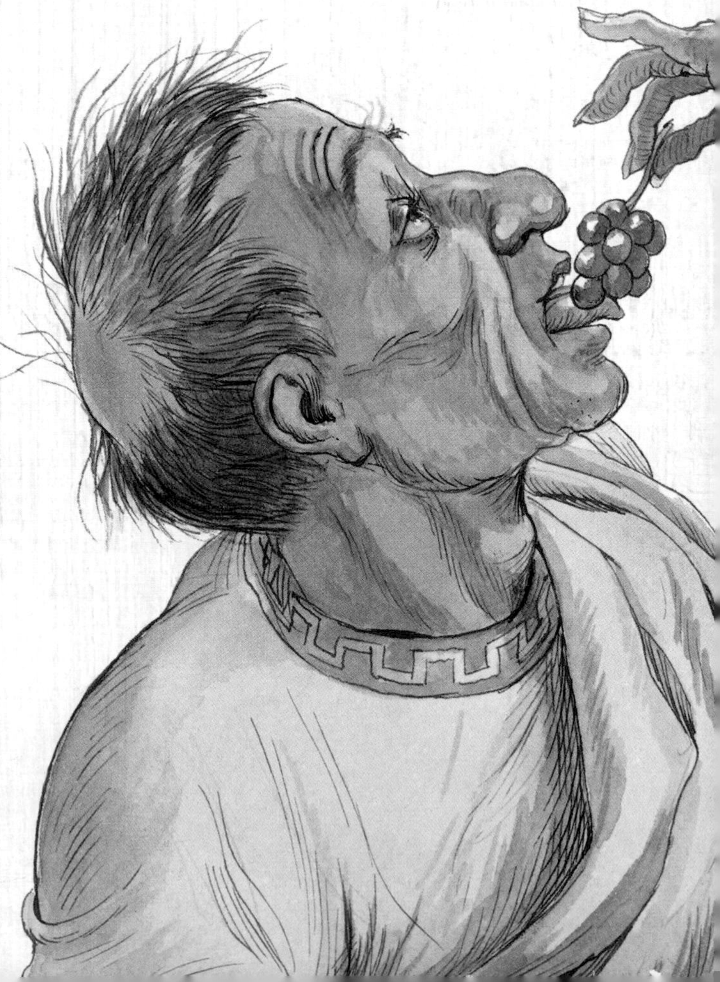

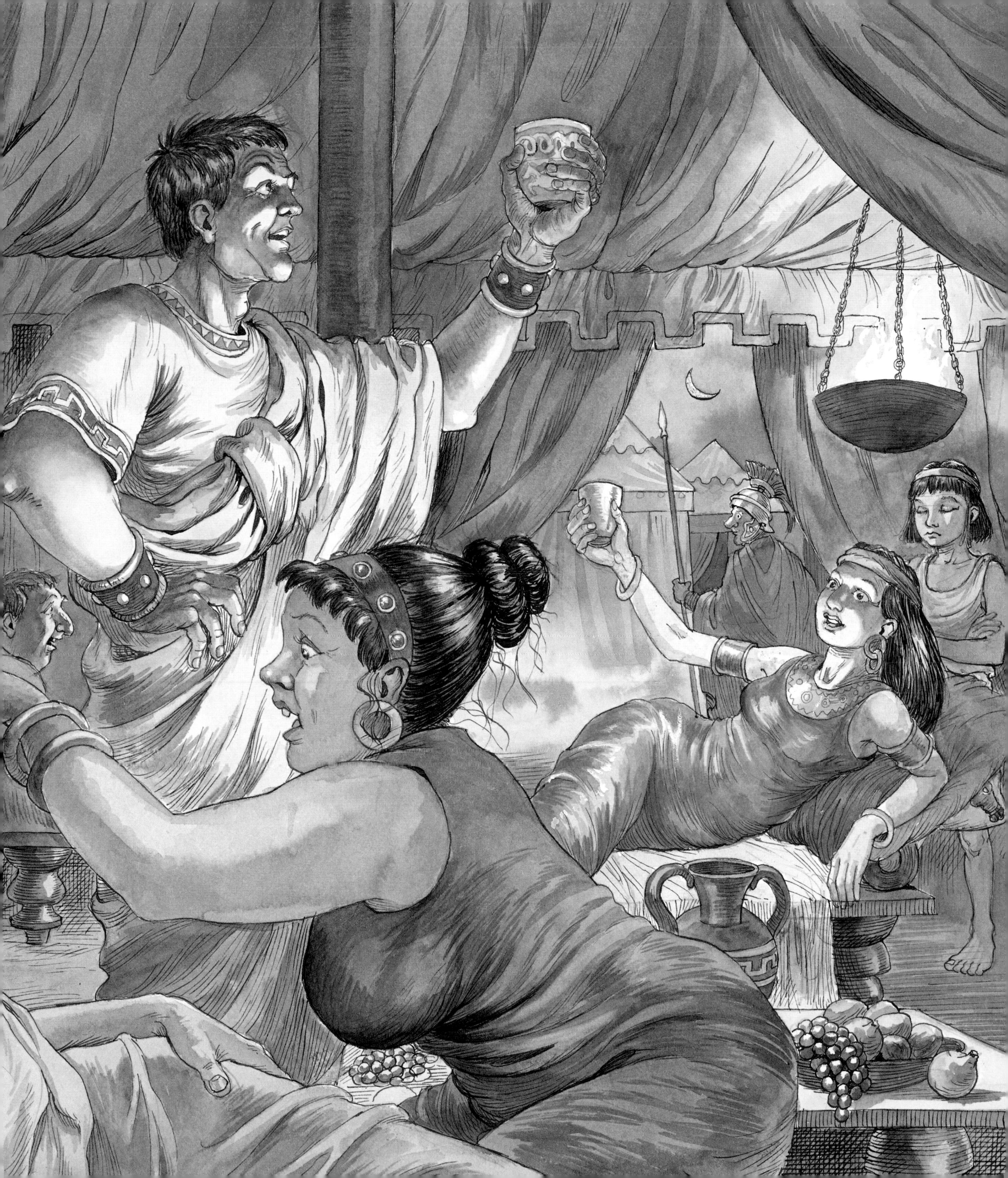

# Morning

## Eleventh Month. Half Moon.

*Marc Antony hasn't gone back to Rome! He is spending the whole winter with Cleopatra in Alexandria.*

We've been back in Alexandria for a while now, and I've had so much to tell my mother. Lotus must have missed me because she follows me everywhere and even wanted to curl up on this papyrus, but I chased her off. She's now sulking on a cushion at my elbow and I can write freely.

The queen brought Marc Antony back with us to Egypt, even though he has a wife in Rome! My mother shrugged her shoulders yesterday when I visited and told her the news. 'She's an enchantress. I've always told you so. There isn't a man alive who doesn't fall under her spell.'

*Some royal servants do not approve of the queen's behaviour with Marc Antony.*

My mother was right. The queen and Marc Antony are deeply in love. Everyone in the palace can see that. They do everything together: riding, hunting, eating, drinking and even going about the city in disguise, playing tricks on unsuspecting people! The older servants never stop tutting and sighing but there isn't anything they can do to stop it. Cleopatra always does exactly what she wants to do. I haven't told anyone this, but yesterday I heard someone whispering that the queen is expecting another baby. I wonder what Caesarion will think about having a little brother or sister? I love my sister, even though she was often a nuisance when she was younger.

# Before The Morning Meal

## Twelfth Month. Three-Quarter Moon.

Today the queen has decided she wants to go with Marc Antony to watch him exercising his troops. I wonder what the Roman soldiers will think about that?

All her servants had to rise early to make sure she was clothed for outdoors and that her make-up was just right for the hot sun. The palace cooks were busy again preparing food for the day. One of the older servants told me that Marc Antony has a huge army – and that many of its legions are here in Egypt.

I don't understand it. How can Marc Antony be living in Egypt with Cleopatra, when he is one of the rulers of another country? I am going to ask Rami if he can try and explain it to me. His father, as a scribe, will know all about it, as he has to write all the official messages for the queen.

Now Cleopatra has departed for the day, I can have my morning meal, and so can Lotus Blossom, who always seems to be hungry. Then we can go and find Rami – I hope he will have time to spend with me today.

*Although he is a Roman general, Marc Antony keeps part of his army in Egypt.*

# Just Before Sunset

## First month. Full moon.

Rami has told me what he knows about Marc Antony and Rome. He said that Marc Antony rules the Roman empire with two other men, Octavian and Lepidus. But while Marc Antony is in Egypt, Octavian thinks he is the real ruler – especially as his uncle was the great Roman general, Julius Caesar. Octavian wants to be the most powerful man in Rome, so Marc Antony's wife, Fulvia, is trying to protect her husband's interests while he's away. I wonder if she knows that her husband is in love with Cleopatra? I don't think I would be so nice to Rami, if he decided to move away from me.

Life at the palace is never dull. Visitors come from all over the world, and rooms for them have to be prepared. In the evenings, when guests are in the palace, the queen fills the halls with music-makers who play flutes and drums and pipes and there are dancers to entertain her friends. I sometimes stand behind a pillar and watch the festivities. One night, Cleopatra ordered the palace cooks to roast twelve pigs, but at different times. This was so that one of the pigs would be ready for whenever Marc Antony wanted it. How the cooks feasted that night on the food that was left over. I think they must have given Lotus some scraps, because she is getting fat!

*The cooks roasted twelve pigs at different times, so Marc Antony could eat when he wanted.*

# Just After Sunrise

## Second Month. Quarter Moon.

The queen is furious. A messenger came for Marc Antony yesterday, saying that he must return to Rome because Fulvia needs his help to fight off Octavian. We could all hear Cleopatra shouting at Marc Antony. 'But what about me? I need you here. I am queen of Egypt and I demand that you stay with me.' But he has gone and we are all very nervous about what might happen...

# After The Midday Meal

## Second Month. Half Moon.

The queen is no longer furious. She has heard that Marc Antony's wife died before he got back to Rome. Cleopatra is happy, because he will be free to marry her and they can rule Rome and Egypt together! Now she is calling me to make her up as the goddess Aphrodite. She wants to look beautiful for when Marc Antony returns. Since the trip to Tarsus, I have been taking care of the queen's jewellery, which is a great responsibility. I also have to make sure that the salves and ointments she uses on her face are always clean and ready to use.

There are red ointments to make her lips shine and black kohl with which she draws lines around her eyes. Her hair oil, which is made from crushed coconuts, is kept in glass bottles and these have to be kept very clean. Her perfumes are kept in pottery phials so that the light will not reach them and spoil them. Cleopatra smells of sandalwood and cypress wood and crushed roses. You can always tell when she's been in a room.

The queen's happiness did not last long. Another messenger came from Rome with bad news. I heard the queen asking him whether he was sure, and whether he'd got the message right. But he had. Marc Antony is not coming back. He has to stay in Rome and, what's worse, he has married someone else. His new wife is Octavia, Octavian's sister. Cleopatra knows that Antony does not love Octavia, it's just one of those 'marriages of convenience' my mother told me about. But it means he won't be with Cleopatra when her baby is born. How sad for her.

All her servants are going to try and cheer her up. We will dance for her, and play cheerful music. The queen loves beautiful things around her and we will all make sure she has them.

# Early Morning

## Seventh Month. Waning Moon.

I have had little time to write. Cleopatra is nearing the end of her pregnancy and she has grown more demanding. She is still furious with Marc Antony, and angry that she can no longer fit into her favourite clothes. Even though there are many robes that will cover her stomach, she is still cross and fretful most of the time. It must be hard to be so heavy in this heat.

They say the queen is having two babies, which means Caesarion will have two little brothers, or sisters, or one of each. I don't think he will like that at all. He is used to being his mother's favourite.

Lotus is also getting heavy – that's because she is having kittens! I thought the cooks were just giving her too many scraps again, but when I felt her tummy I could feel something moving around. I wonder how many kittens she will have?

I haven't the time to see my friends as much as I used to and Rami only visits the palace every few days. We used to walk by the river in the evenings, but there's no time to do that nowadays. Maybe when we're married, we'll be able to. My mother tells me that Nanu and Sheriti are both to be married next month... before me!

*Marc Antony has not returned to Egypt, even though he knows Cleopatra is pregnant.*

# Late Evening

## Eighth month. Half moon.

The day before yesterday, at the end of the seventh month, the queen gave birth to twins: a boy and a girl. Their names are to be Alexander Helios (Helios is the Greek word for 'sun') and Cleopatra Selene (Selene is the Greek word for 'moon'). Everyone in the palace is rejoicing. Word has been sent to Marc Antony. I wonder if he will come back to Egypt? Everyone is saying that his new wife in Rome, Octavia, will not be nearly as happy as we are here in Egypt.

Lotus has had her kittens! She is the happy mother of three lovely little ones.

Two kittens are black. The other one is exactly the same colour as the amber in a bracelet the queen gave me for cheering her up when Marc Antony went back to Rome. So that's what I've named her: Amber. The queen gives her babies to a wet nurse to be fed, but Lotus feeds her kittens herself and seems to enjoy it.

Lotus and her kittens have been shut out of the palace nursery, of course. Everyone knows that cats love to jump into infants' cradles and go to sleep among the soft blankets that are always to be found there. Though the queen seems to love the kittens as much as she loves her babies.

In a few months' time I will be leaving the queen's service, because I need to return home to prepare for my marriage. I am a little nervous about this, but it will be much easier for me than for girls who hardly know their husbands when they marry. I am going to be Rami's wife. I am already good at writing, but he will be able to teach me even more.

# Before The Evening Meal

## Twelfth month. Full moon.

The queen called me to her chamber this morning and said, 'Nefret, my pretty one, you are a woman now. You must marry and have your own children. You have been a loyal handmaiden to me, but now it is time for your own life. But I have a favour to ask of you. Will you let me keep the three little cats at the palace? One for each of my children?'

How could I refuse the queen of Egypt? (I don't think Lotus will be very happy for a while as she will miss her little ones.)

I know I shall enjoy being Rami's wife for we are such good friends. And we'll still live near the palace so can visit there often. My cousin Iras, who is much younger than me, will take my place here soon and when she does, I'll be able to guide her and teach her what she needs to know. I've learned so much from the queen and even though the work has been hard, I have enjoyed being in her presence and being her Nefret, her 'pretty one'.

# What happened next?

Marc Antony did not return to Alexandria for four years. He went to live in Greece with Octavia, and she had two children. Then, three years after Nefret left the palace – in the year we now call 37BCE, Antony left his wife, Octavia, to return to his real love, Cleopatra. It was the first time he had met his twin children. He married Cleopatra in an Egyptian ceremony and they had another child, Ptolemy Philadelphus.

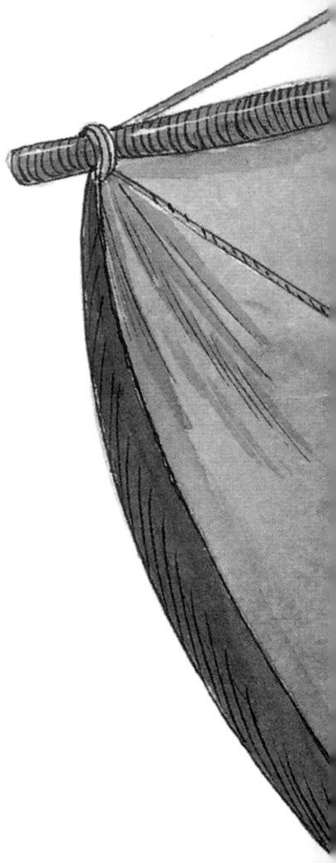

Now it was Octavia's turn to be furious because Antony had abandoned her and their two daughters. She went to her brother, Octavian, who persuaded the Romans to declare war on Egypt. Octavian and Antony had always been bitter rivals, so Octavian didn't hesitate.

In 31BCE, Antony fought a sea battle against them at Actium, in Greece. Cleopatra sent some ships of her own to help Antony, but the Romans won this battle. When Cleopatra saw that Antony's forces were defeated, she fled, and Antony followed her. This made the Romans think that he was unable to act on his own and was simply following where Cleopatra led him.

In 30BCE, Octavian reached Alexandria. Cleopatra had been learning how to make poisons and experimenting to see which would bring death most swiftly and painlessly. She had also had a huge tomb-like chamber built and when this mausoleum was ready, she moved her precious treasures into it.

After another sea battle, Marc Antony was convinced that Cleopatra had betrayed him and was now on the Romans' side. She fled to her mausoleum, with her maidservants, Iras and Charmian, because she was sure that Marc Antony would try to kill her for what he thought was her treacherous behaviour.

Cleopatra ordered her servants to tell Marc Antony that she was dead. Marc Antony believed this and begged one of his servants, Eros, to kill him. Eros killed himself instead, not wanting to harm his master. Marc Antony wept for the loss of his faithful attendant, and stabbed himself with his own dagger, but he succeeded only in wounding himself very badly.

Cleopatra found out what had happened and asked to see Marc Antony. He was overjoyed that she was still alive and he had himself taken to the mausoleum. He was hauled up through the window because the door was locked against the Romans. Cleopatra was distraught when she saw that her beloved Marc Antony was dying. She laid him on her own bed and called him husband and lord. Marc Antony died, asking her to remember only the happy times they had shared.

Octavian allowed Cleopatra to arrange Marc Antony's funeral. She buried him with royal splendour and then retired to her bed, saying she wanted nothing more than to join him in death. Octavian guarded her very closely, fearing that she intended to take her own life, but Cleopatra persuaded him in the end that she was feeling better and could be allowed to return to the mausoleum.

Once she was safely back among her own servants, Cleopatra took a bath and ordered a feast. While this was being prepared, a man arrived at the gates with a basket of figs. Cleopatra's guards checked the basket and found nothing suspicious in it. After the feast, the queen wrote a letter to Octavian, sealed it and sent a messenger to deliver it to him. The letter asked Octavian to allow her to be buried in Marc Antony's tomb. Octavian realized that this meant Cleopatra intended to kill herself and he sent soldiers to the mausoleum at once. They arrived too late. Cleopatra was dead on her bed. The soldiers found two pinpricks on the queen's arm and the story grew that she had allowed herself to be bitten by an asp, an extremely poisonous snake, which had been hidden in the basket of figs all along.
She was buried, as she had wished,
beside her beloved Marc Antony.

# Cleopatra's Family Tree

**Cleopatra was a member of the Ptolemy family. The first Ptolemy was Macedonian and one of Alexander the Great's generals. When Alexander died in 323BCE, Ptolemy decided he would be the ruler of Egypt and become Ptolemy I. Instead of being a soldier, he would become a god-king.**

But as Ptolemy was a god-king, he could not marry an ordinary woman – he had to marry one of his own family. That is why all the Ptolemies married their sisters (or in Cleopatra's case, her brothers). The children of the Ptolemies were all called Ptolemy or Cleopatra (except for Cleopatra's children, but that's because they had Roman fathers, rather than Ptolemy fathers).

Cleopatra was the last queen of Egypt. After her death, Egypt became a Roman province. Her son, Caesarion, was murdered by his own tutor, on Octavian's orders. Octavian was worried that Caesarion might grow up to be a threat because he was Julius Caesar's son. Cleopatra's other three children were sent to Rome where they were raised by Octavia, Marc Antony's Roman widow.

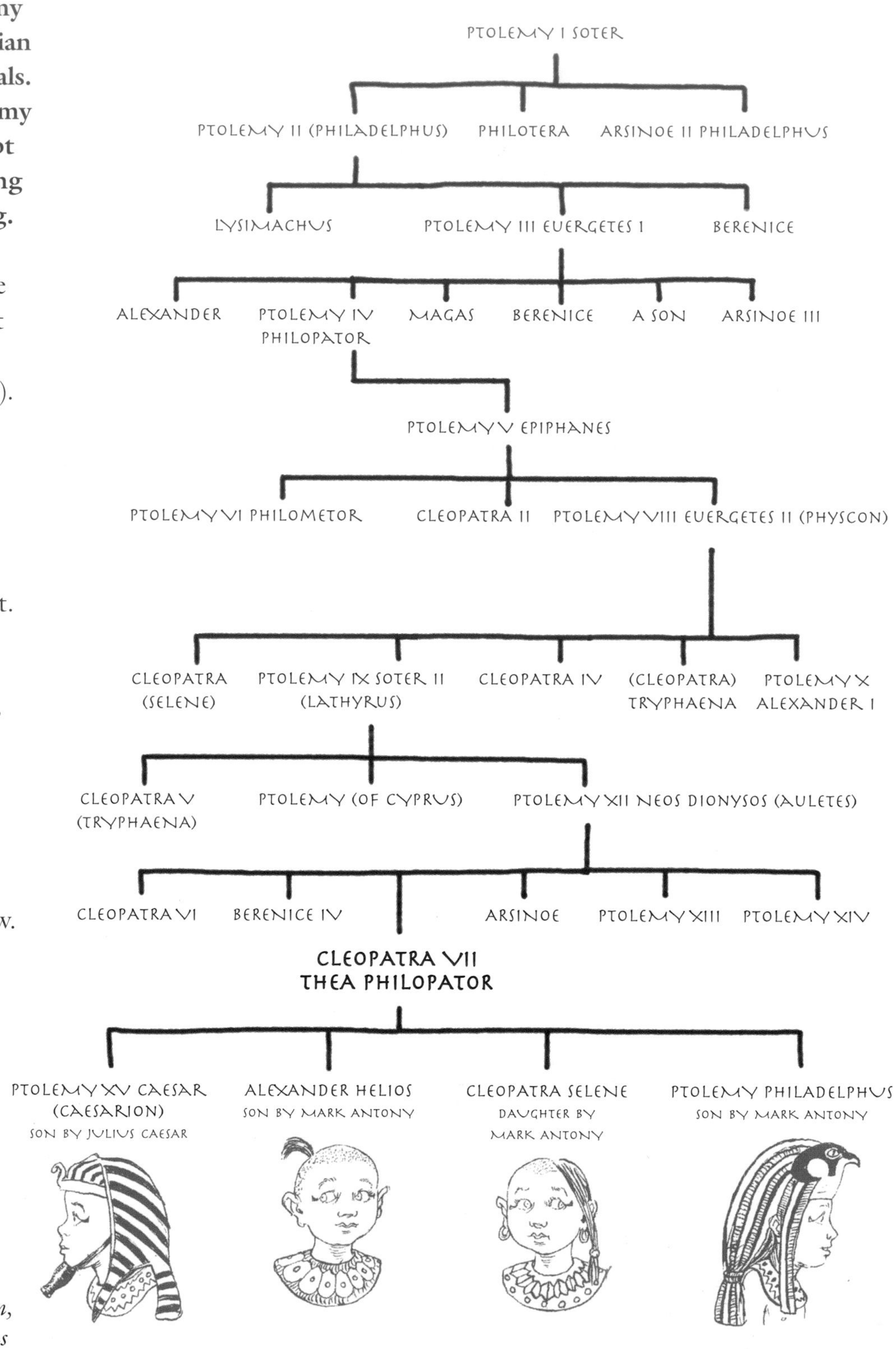


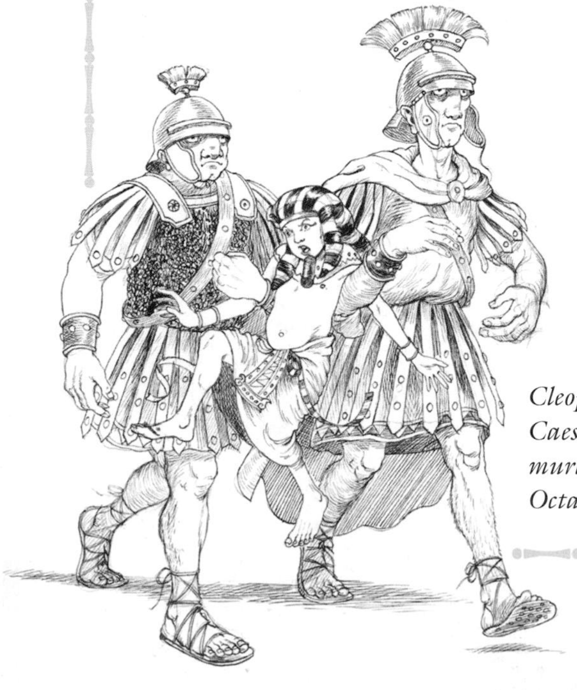

*Cleopatra's son, Caesarion, was murdered on Octavian's orders.*

# NEFRET'S WORLD

**Though Nefret's diary is a story, the places, people and events she writes about are real. Egypt was one of the most famous civilizations of the ancient world and it had been in existence for almost 4,000 years before Nefret was born. The pyramids and great temples had been built about 3,000 years earlier, so for Nefret, they were ancient history.**

For its final 1,000 years, Egypt was conquered in turn by different peoples: the Assyrians, the Parthians, the Greeks and the Romans. Nefret lived to see the end of the ancient Egyptian era.

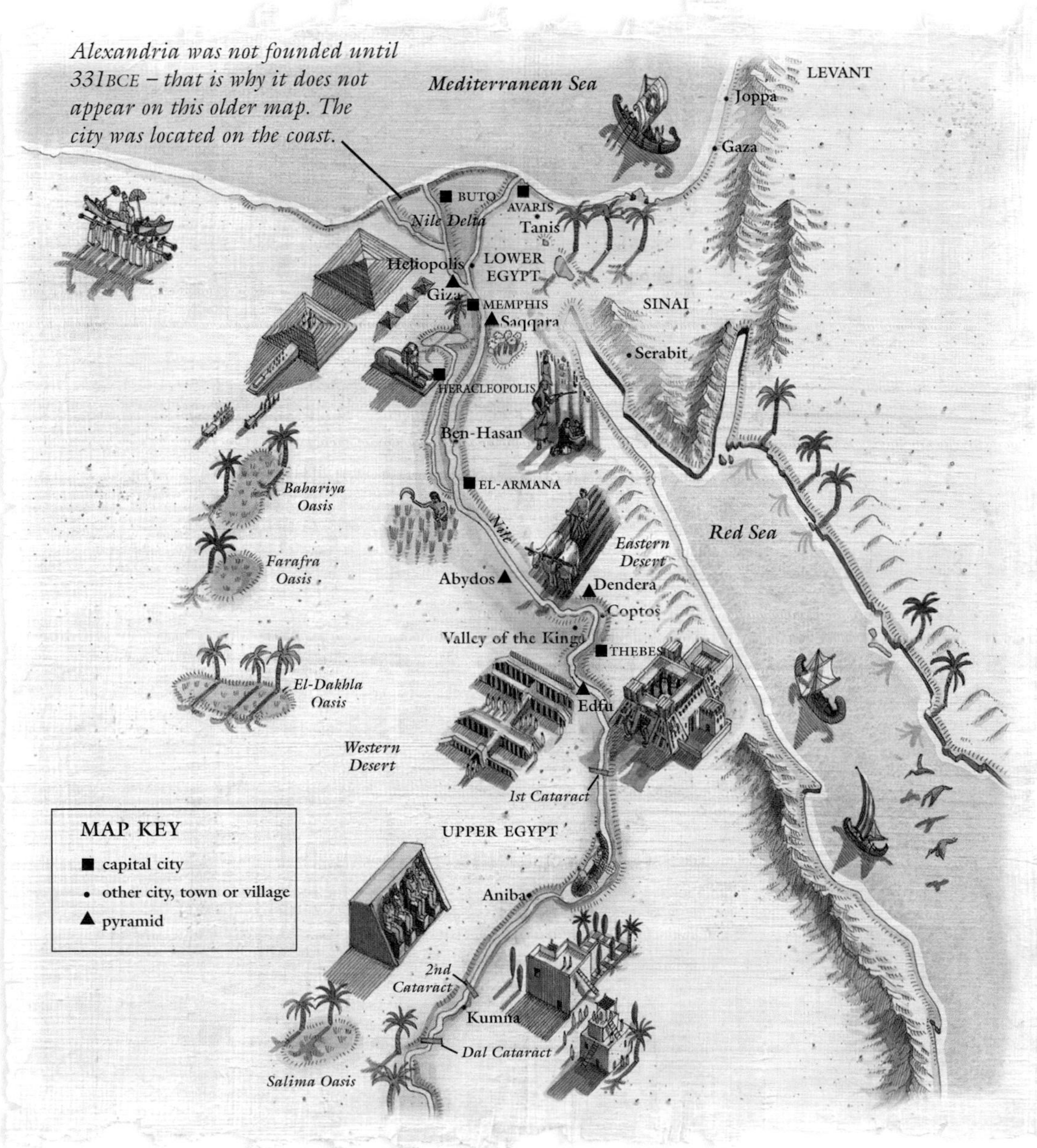


## ANCIENT EGYPT TIMELINE

**3500BCE**

**3500** Farming flourishes in the Nile Valley

**3300** First Egyptian towns built

**3300–3000** Hieroglyphic script is developed

**3000BCE**

**3000** Upper and Lower Egypt united with capital at Memphis

**2920** First dynasty of kings begins to rule

**2630** First step pyramid built at Saqqara

**2575** Sneferu founds 4th dynasty and establishes powerful Old Kingdom based at Memphis

**2550** Khufu builds Great Pyramid at Giza

**2500BCE**

**2134** Old Kingdom ends as Egypt divides into two rival kingdoms

**2040** Egypt reunified under 11th dynasty, establishing the Middle Kingdom

**2000BCE**

**1640–1550** Hyksos people from the Levant conquer and rule Lower Egypt

**1550** Ahmose founds 18th dynasty and establishes New Kingdom

**1500BCE**

**1473–1458** Hatshepsut is queen and sends naval expedition to Punt in east Africa

**1353–1335** Akhenaten creates a short-lived monotheistic (one-god) religion based on Aten, the sun-god

**1333–1323** Reign of Tutankhamun, the boy pharaoh

**1290–1224** Rameses II extends Egyptian empire into the Levant

**1070** Fall of 21st dynasty marks end of effective Egyptian power

**1000BCE**

**671–651** Assyrians occupy Egypt

**525–523** Persians briefly conquer Egypt

**500BCE**

**332** Alexander the Great conquers Egypt, establishing a new Ptolemaic dynasty

**30** Death of Cleopatra, last Egyptian pharaoh; Egypt becomes part of Roman empire

**0**

**The Pharos Lighthouse**
*This lighthouse was one of the seven wonders of the ancient world. It was built on an island connected to the mainland by a wide causeway called the Heptastadion. Built on the orders of Ptolemy II to guide ships into port, the lighthouse was 130m tall. It had a huge fire at the top, which could be seen as far out at sea as 50km.*

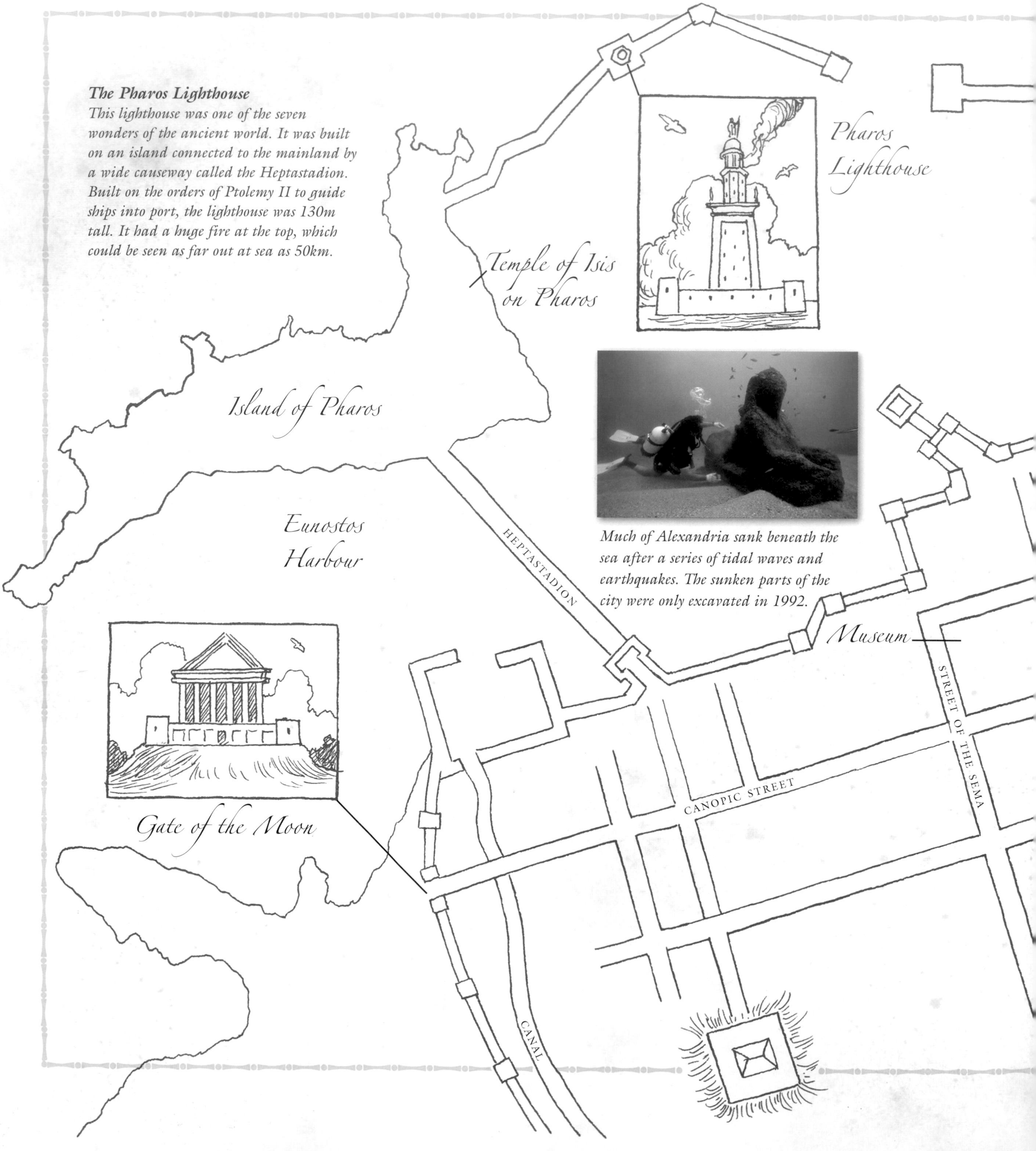


*Much of Alexandria sank beneath the sea after a series of tidal waves and earthquakes. The sunken parts of the city were only excavated in 1992.*

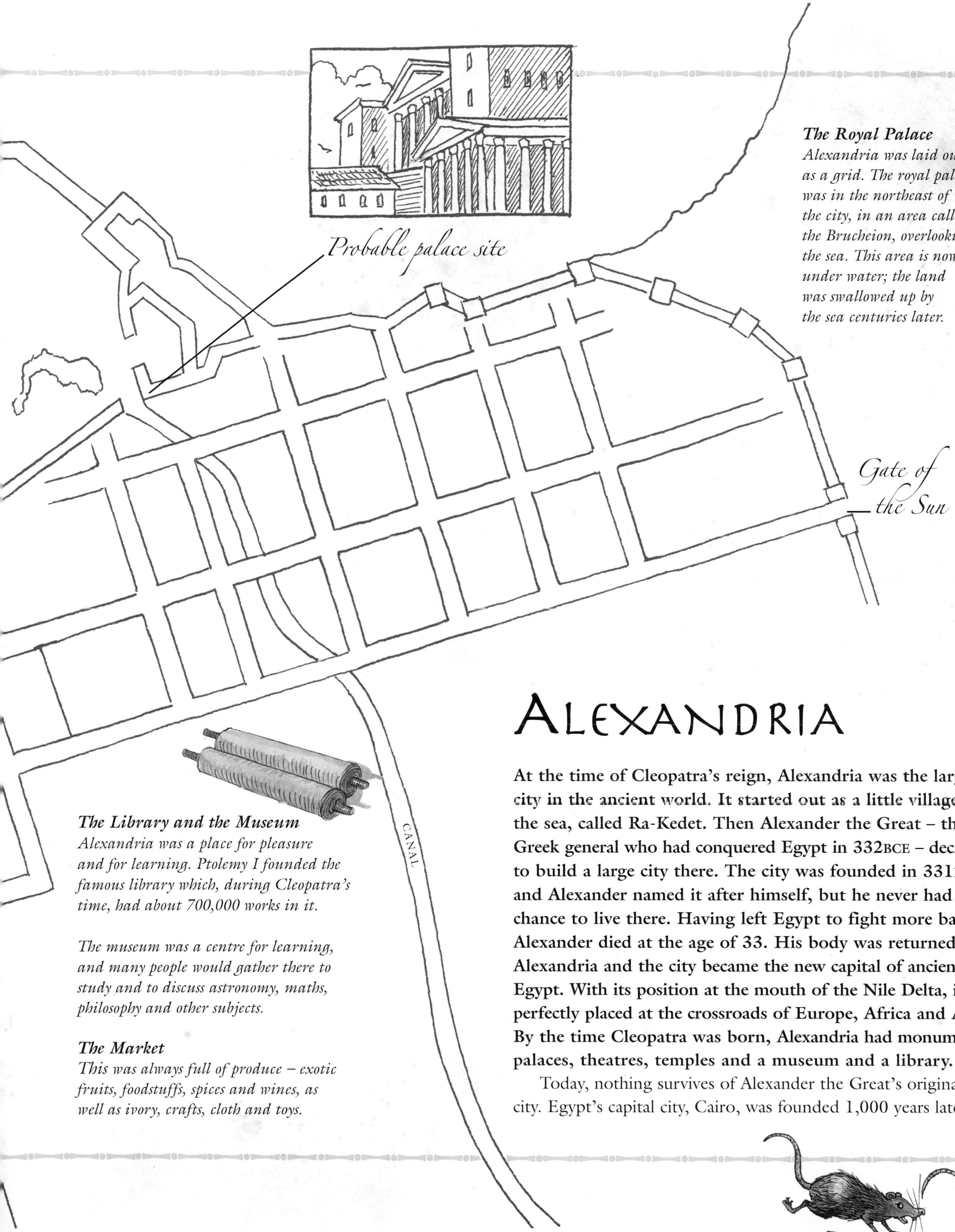


**The Royal Palace**
*Alexandria was laid out as a grid. The royal palace was in the northeast of the city, in an area called the Brucheion, overlooking the sea. This area is now under water; the land was swallowed up by the sea centuries later.*

**The Library and the Museum**
*Alexandria was a place for pleasure and for learning. Ptolemy I founded the famous library which, during Cleopatra's time, had about 700,000 works in it.*

*The museum was a centre for learning, and many people would gather there to study and to discuss astronomy, maths, philosophy and other subjects.*

**The Market**
*This was always full of produce – exotic fruits, foodstuffs, spices and wines, as well as ivory, crafts, cloth and toys.*

# ALEXANDRIA

**At the time of Cleopatra's reign, Alexandria was the largest city in the ancient world. It started out as a little village on the sea, called Ra-Kedet. Then Alexander the Great – the Greek general who had conquered Egypt in 332BCE – decided to build a large city there. The city was founded in 331BCE and Alexander named it after himself, but he never had a chance to live there. Having left Egypt to fight more battles, Alexander died at the age of 33. His body was returned to Alexandria and the city became the new capital of ancient Egypt. With its position at the mouth of the Nile Delta, it was perfectly placed at the crossroads of Europe, Africa and Asia. By the time Cleopatra was born, Alexandria had monuments, palaces, theatres, temples and a museum and a library.**

Today, nothing survives of Alexander the Great's original city. Egypt's capital city, Cairo, was founded 1,000 years later.

# The People

**Alexandria was a crowded city with many different communities. Three main groups of people lived there: the Greeks who lived in the centre of the city; the Jews who lived in the east of the city, and the Egyptians – the poorest group – who lived in the old city in the west. There were also thousands of travellers who passed through Alexandria: there were traders and camel caravans from Africa and Asia, and seafarers from all over the world, bringing goods and armies to Egypt.**

*Linen is made from a plant called flax. The Egyptians spun and wove it into lengths of light cloth for clothing.*

**Hair**

Hairstyles were very important to girls and women in ancient Egypt. They wore their hair in different ways: long, curly, ruffled or plaited into small braids and decorated with ribbons and flowers. Young servant girls would often wear their hair in thin plaits, with fragrant incense cones on their heads. These would melt slowly in the heat, and a wonderful scent would surround them.

**Clothing**

Clothes were very simple and young children were often naked. Girls and women from richer families wore clothing made from white linen, which became finer and more see-through over the centuries. Their outer garments were often pleated, and belts, jewellery and thin shawls were often worn to add colour. Jewellery was not just for wealthy women; wealthy men wore plenty too.

**Beauty and make-up**

Because Egypt was a hot and dry country, the ancient Egyptians had to use plenty of moisturiser to keep their skin feeling soft. The poor used castor oil, but the rich used scented oils which often took around six months to produce. Fresh incense under the arms was an effective ancient Egyptian deodorant. Men *and* women wore make-up. Eyes had to be large and almond-shaped with different colours being fashionable at different times.

*Young boys and girls wore their hair in 'sidelock of youth' until they were about ten years old.*

# The Roman Army

**During Cleopatra's reign, there were many Roman soldiers living in Alexandria. Julius Caesar left behind three legions of them to look after her when he returned to Rome. Each legion was made up of infantrymen called legionaries, the soldiers in charge of them, called centurions, and the generals in charge of each legion. There was also the cavalry, who were soldiers on horseback, and auxiliaries – neither of these two divisions were Roman citizens.**

Soldiers were trained to fight together. They marched into battle in a line with their shields next to each other. If the enemy shot arrows at them, the soldiers in the rows behind the front line would lift their shields over their heads like a roof to protect them. This was called a testudo, which means 'tortoise'.

Life for Roman soldiers away from home could be quite lonely. Some mothers would send their sons letters and parcels from Italy to stop them feeling so homesick!

*Marc Antony's army went into battle against Octavian with as many as 75,000 legionaries, 25,000 auxiliaries and 12,000 cavalry in it.*

*To show the difference in rank, some centurions carried a stick which they used to beat any soldier who disobeyed an order. The important centurions also wore special armour, which emphasized their rank.*

# The River Nile

**The River Nile flows right through the middle of Egypt. Starting from the mountains of central Africa, the river runs all the way to the Mediterranean Sea. When the snows melt in the mountains, the river flows faster. Every spring the Nile used to flood (before the Aswan Dam was completed in the 1970s), with the water spreading for kilometres. When the flood waters drained away, it left behind rich, fertile soil.**

**Farming**

Farmers dug canals to take the water from the river for their crops. They grew grain to make bread, flax to make cloth, grapes to make wine, as well as other fruits and vegetables. Their cattle would graze on the land and from them they would get meat, milk and leather – they had everything they needed. But that depended on the river flooding each year. If it didn't, there was a drought year meaning there was no harvest and, therefore, no food.

**Food**

The Egyptians liked to eat three times a day. The morning meal was called 'mouthwashing' and it was usually taken alone. The midday and evening meals, called 'the rising of the stars', were eaten with family and friends. Tomb paintings show that Egyptians ate all sorts of fruits, vegetables, meat and fish. They baked 35 different sorts of bread and cakes. Ordinary Egyptians drank a thick beer made from grain. The beer was brewed at home. Richer people drank sweet wine that was served in jugs.

**Papyrus**

Nefret tells us that she wrote on rolls of papyrus. Papyrus is a plant that grew in the marshes around the River Nile and the thick stems were used to make many things: ropes, baskets and sometimes even boats. But most importantly, they were used to make a type of writing material. The stems were cut into strips and the strips laid on top of each other to make sheets. One scroll was called a papyrus, two or more scrolls were called papyri. The sheets – usually in squares – were fixed together to make a roll. If you were poor, you would write on both sides.

**The calendar**

The earliest Egyptian calendar was based on the annual flooding of the River Nile. The Egyptians divided the year into 12 months and three seasons: akhet (the flooding), peret (spring, when the crops grew) and shemu (harvest time). Each season consisted of four 30-day months; each month had three ten-day weeks. Day and night were divided into 12 hours each.

During Nefret's time, Julius Caesar made changes to the calendar and the Julian calendar was developed, which is the basis of our modern calendar.

*Papyrus was a precious resource and the ancient Egyptians knew how to recycle it. Many surviving letters written on papyrus were 'palimpsest' – that is, written on top of an earlier letter.*

# Children and Education

**Nefret tells us she had older brothers and a little sister, Kebi. Most families in ancient Egypt had four or five children who lived beyond adolescence. They would also have had more babies who died during childbirth or shortly after.**

*There were over 3,000 hieroglyphic signs, and 800 were regularly used. To become a scribe, you would have had to learn at least 700 hieroglyphs.*

Most children in ancient Egypt, and the majority of Egyptian adults, could not read or write. Boys learned the trades of their fathers and took over from them when they could no longer work. Boys from the upper classes of Egyptian society learned to read and write, and also learned mathematics. Such boys would probably have been taught in scribal schools attached to a temple or palace.

Girls learned domestic skills like cooking and weaving from their mothers. They had no formal education and were unlikely to be able to read and write. There were exceptions, however, as letters written by women were found. Some, like Nefret, may have learned this skill from a scribe who was a family friend.

*Learning was by rote – repeating things over and over again until they were memorised. The teachers were very strict. One surviving text says, 'A boy's ear is on his back – he listens when he is beaten.'*

**Writing**

Nefret was very lucky to have a friend like Rami to teach her to write, because it was very unusual for girls in ancient Egypt to be able to do this. Most people think of hieroglyphics when they think of ancient Egyptian writing. But this form of writing had virtually died out by Cleopatra's time, except for religious carvings and the official writing of the royal name. Non-religious writing on papyrus scrolls used demotic script.

*Reed pens were made by cutting and shaping a single reed straw or length of bamboo. They were the most common writing implement during Cleopatra's time. The scribe kept his pens in a palette made from wood or ivory.*

*The text on the Rosetta Stone (now on display at the British Museum in London) – dated 27 March 196BCE – tells of the good things that Ptolemy V had done for Egypt.*

**The Rosetta Stone**

This shows the same piece of writing in hieroglyphic, demotic and Greek. It was only when this stone was discovered in 1799CE in the village of el-Rashid (Rosetta) that Egyptologists were able to begin to decipher Egyptian hieroglyphics. The names of Ptolemy and Cleopatra were deciphered on the stone first. Later – in 1822CE – these words provided the Egyptologist Jean-François Champollion with the means to understand hieroglyphics.

# Pharaohs, Pyramids and Religion

**Pharaohs were the rulers of ancient Egypt – kings and queens. The word comes from per-aa meaning 'great house', and describes the royal court rather than the person. The Egyptians believed that their rulers were gods, or children of gods. Cleopatra thought of herself as the goddess Isis. She was the last queen of ancient Egypt.**

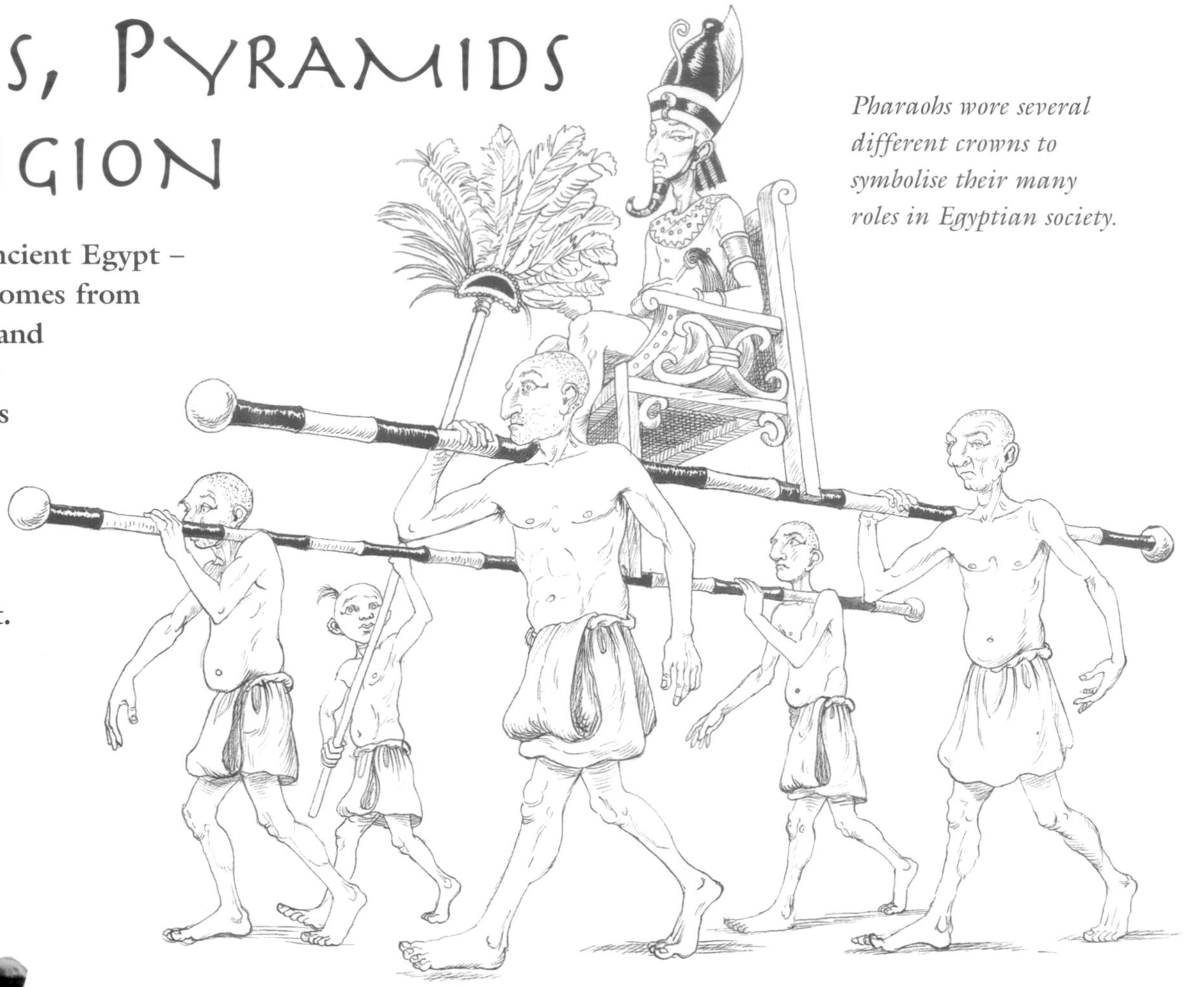

*Pharaohs wore several different crowns to symbolise their many roles in Egyptian society.*

*In Egyptian temples, Cleopatra (below) had herself portrayed with all the attributes of a pharaoh, as the goddess Isis come down to earth.*

*Tutankhamun has become far more famous in death than he ever was in his lifetime. His funerary mask (right) is one of the most famous Egyptian images.*

**Two famous pharaohs**

Tutankhamun was pharaoh between 1336–1327BCE. He was only about eight years old when he became ruler of ancient Egypt. His tomb was discovered in the Valley of the Kings in 1922CE.

Hatshepsut was a famous female pharaoh who ruled from about 1479–1458BCE. She is known as 'the woman who reigned as a man' and is often depicted with a royal beard. She had a tomb built in the Valley of the Kings, but was never buried there.

**The Valley of the Kings**
This was the main royal cemetery of ancient Egypt. There are 62 tombs there. The smallest tomb in the valley is Tutankhamun's. The valley had stopped being used well before the Ptolemies ruled Egypt. Cleopatra was buried with Marc Antony but their tomb has never been found.

*Pyramids were built high to help the pharaoh's spirit rise to the stars. They were constructed from stone, to protect the pharaoh's embalmed body and to house his or her precious belongings, needed for the afterlife. There were two types – the 'step pyramid' (above) and the 'true pyramid' (below).*

*The Great Pyramid at Giza is the largest surviving pyramid. It was built by Khufu, son of Sneferu.*

# Gods and Goddesses

**In temple carvings and paintings, statues and mummy cases, the gods are shown in different forms. Sometimes they appear as humans, sometimes as humans with the heads of animals or birds, and sometimes solely as animals. The Egyptians had hundreds of gods and goddesses.**

*The major gods and goddesses*

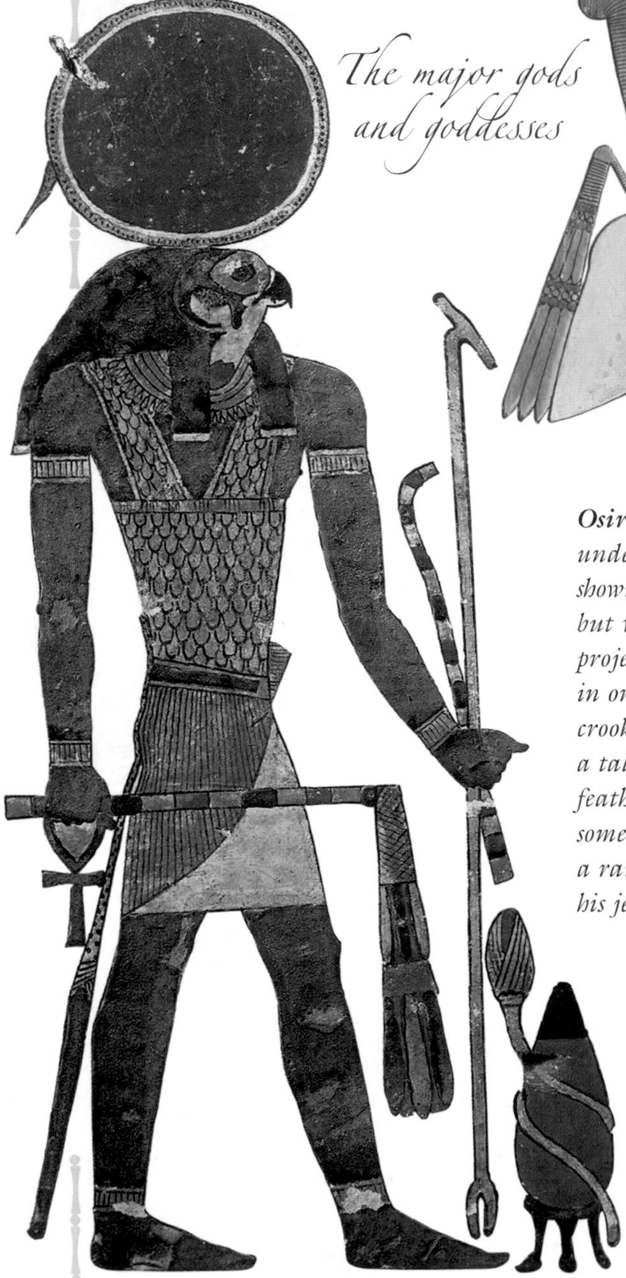

*Ra (or Re)* is the sun god and 'father' of all pharaohs. He is usually depicted with a human body and a falcon's head, on which was a sun and a sacred asp.

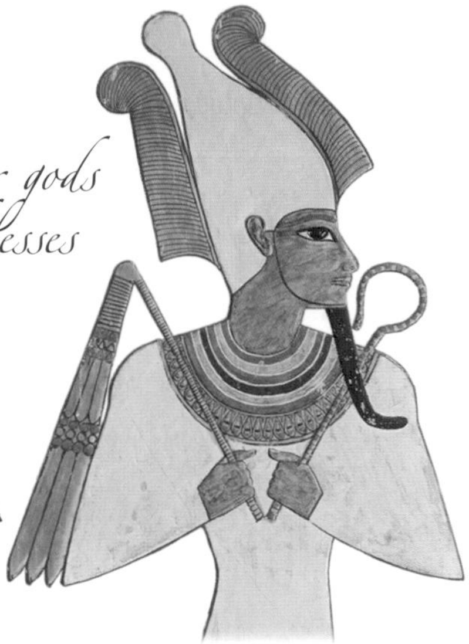

***Osiris*** *is the ruler of the underworld. He is usually shown wrapped as a mummy, but with his hands projecting from the cloths in order to hold the royal crook and flail. He wears a tall white crown with feathers on either side, and sometimes with the horns of a ram. Osiris was killed by his jealous brother, Seth.*

***Isis*** *is the sister and wife of Osiris. The goddess of the harvest, Isis is usually depicted with a horn and a sun on her head, and wearing beautiful robes. Cleopatra thought of herself as Isis and loved dressing up as her.*

***Horus*** *is the son of Isis. He is sometimes depicted as a falcon, and sometimes as a man with a falcon's head (like Ra). Horus was the god of the sky. In Cleopatra's time, a new image of Horus emerged and small sculptures in wood or stone have been found showing Horus as a naked child-god standing on a crocodile or holding poisonous snakes.*

***Seth*** *is the god of chaos and destruction, and the evil brother of Osiris. Seth is generally shown with a human body but the head of an animal a bit like an anteater. But sometimes he's been represented as a hippopotamus, a pig or a donkey. Seth locked Osiris in a coffin and threw him into the River Nile. Isis found the coffin, but so did Seth, who then made sure he was well and truly dead by chopping him into small pieces.*

**The Afterlife**

The ancient Egyptians did not believe that death was the end of a person's life. People who died needed their bodies so that their spirit, Ka, could return to them after the funeral service.

**Mummies**

In order to preserve a body, the Egyptian embalmers mummified it. The best way of preserving a body was to remove all the internal organs and clean out the inside of the body with wine and spices. Then the body was covered with embalming agents for at least 40 days, to mummify it. After this time the body was wrapped from head to toe in cloth that was soaked in a kind of glue.

*Egyptians believed the journey to the next world should be as smooth as possible. Amulets such as this one were bound into the mummy's layers of linen for good luck.*

**Mummy cases**

The embalmers would give the prepared body back to the relatives, who would place it in a decorated wooden coffin – a mummy case which was shaped like the dead person. The relatives would place the mummy, upright, in a burial chamber together with the person's favourite possessions for life after death.

*Mummification was only for the rich – poorer people were buried in simple graves in the sand, allowing the body to be preserved naturally.*

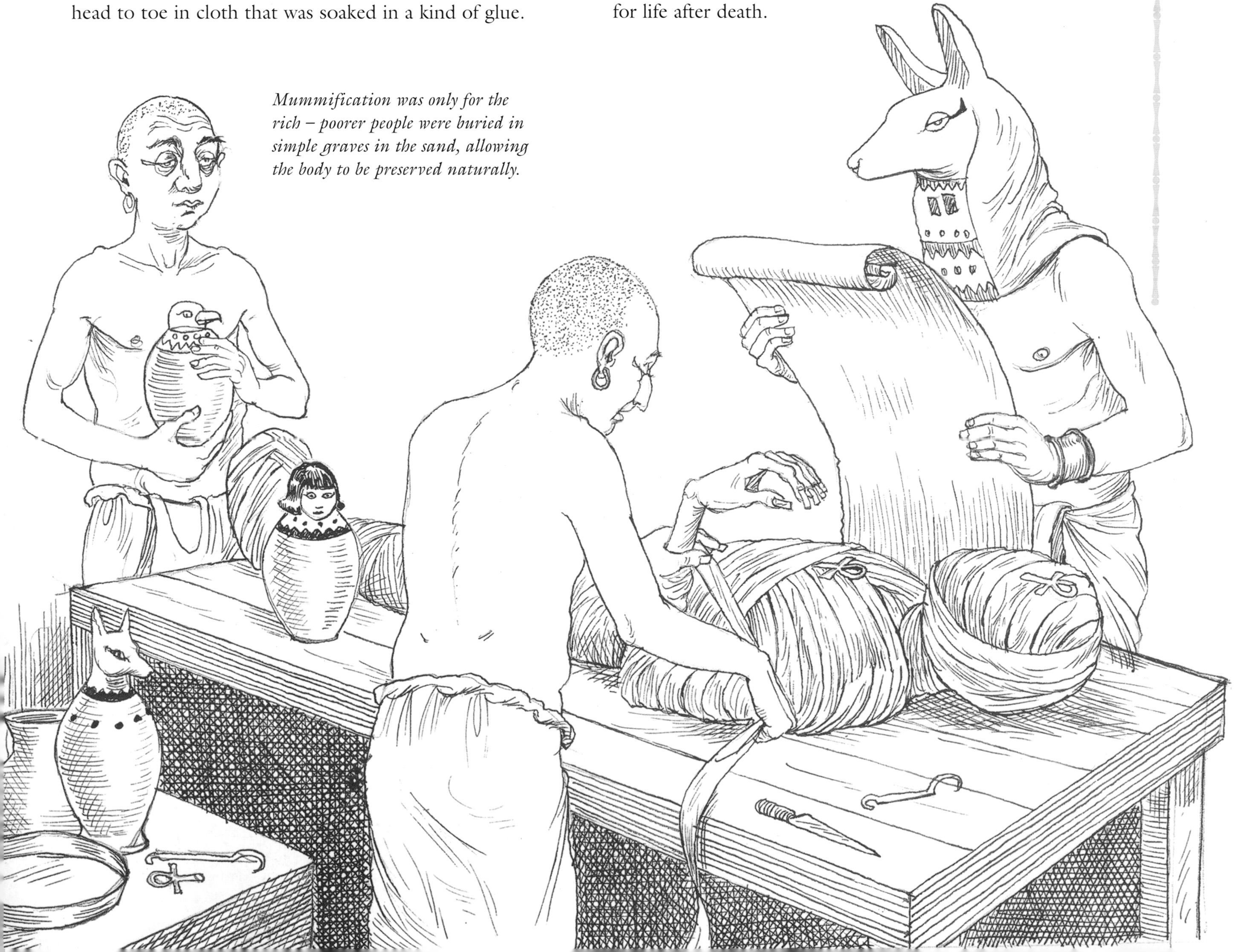

# GLOSSARY

**Alexander the Great**
The king of Macedonia from 336–323BCE, who conquered many lands and is the hero in ancient Greek legends.

**allies**
Countries that are friends or joined by an agreement called a treaty.

**Aphrodite**
The ancient Greek goddess of love and beauty.

**asp**
A poisonous snake, such as the Egyptian cobra, which was a symbol of royalty in ancient Egypt.

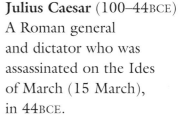

**astrology**
The study of the impact of the stars and planets on people's lives.

**boars**
Wild pigs, or male pigs.

**chamber**
A room, especially a bedroom.

**charms**
Ornaments that are worn because people believe that they bring good luck or ward off evil.

**civil war**
A war between people who live in the same country.

**Cleopatra**
(69–30BCE) There were a number of Egyptian queens called Cleopatra, but the most famous was Cleopatra VII (the Cleopatra who features in this book). She was a lover of Julius Caesar and Marc Antony. She became queen on the death of her father in 51BCE and ruled Egypt with her two brothers, Ptolemy XIII and Ptolemy XIV, and then with her son Ptolemy XV Caesar (Caesarion).

**Cupid**
The ancient Roman god of love.

**delta**
A triangular area at the mouth of a river where material is deposited.

**demotic script**
A type of ancient Egyptian writing that came after picture writing called hieroglyphic script.

**enchantress**
A woman who puts a charm or spell on people.

**floods**
When a river overflows its banks on to land that is normally dry.

**fragrant**
Having a sweet smell.

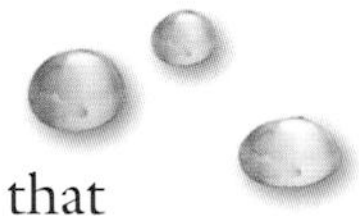

**gemstones**
Precious stones that are used in jewellery.

**generals**
The top ranks of an army.

**grain**
Wheat, barley or oats.

**handmaiden**
A female servant or personal maid.

**harvest**
The time of gathering in ripe crops.

**headdress**
A decorative head covering.

**hieroglyphics**
A system of writing using pictures, used by the ancient Egyptians.

**Horus**
An ancient Egyptian god in the form of a falcon.

**Isis**
An ancient Egyptian goddess who was the wife of Osiris and the mother of Horus.

**jetty**
A landing platform at the side of a river.

**Julius Caesar** (100–44BCE)
A Roman general and dictator who was assassinated on the Ides of March (15 March), in 44BCE.

**kohl**
A mixture of soot and other ingredients used to darken the eyelids and eyelashes.

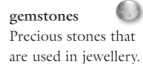

**legion**
A unit of the ancient Roman army made up of between 3,000 and 6,000 soldiers.

**Marc Antony**
(83–30BCE) A Roman general who served under Julius Caesar, and later ruled Rome along with Octavian and Lepidus. He was defeated by Octavian (the future emperor Augustus) and committed suicide with Cleopatra in 30BCE.

**mausoleum**
A tomb above ground.

**merchant traders**
People who buy and sell things for profit.

**papyrus**
An ancient Egyptian paper made from reeds.

**plains**
Large areas of flat land.

**plotting**
Secretly planning.

**Pompey** (106–48BCE)
A Roman general and politician who led Rome with Julius Caesar and Marcus Crassus between 61–54BCE. He was later defeated in battle by Caesar and murdered by Ptolemy XIII.

**port**
A harbour, or town with a harbour.

**Ptolemy XIII** (63–47BCE)
A younger brother of Cleopatra VII who became joint ruler of Egypt with her after their father's death. He died as he tried to flee from Caesar's forces in 47BCE.

**Ptolemy XIV** (59–44BCE)
A younger brother of Cleopatra VII who co-ruled Egypt with his sister until he was killed to make way for her son by Julius Caesar, Ptolemy XV Caesar (Caesarion).

**Roman empire**
An ancient state centred around the city of Rome, which was ruled by emperors until its collapse in 476CE.

**Roman province**
The Roman empire was divided into provinces, which were governed by Roman officials.

**rushlights**
Candles with wicks made from plants called rushes.

**salve**
A soothing substance applied to wounds.

**sandalwood**
A type of tree that has scented wood.

**scribes**
People in ancient Egyptian times whose jobs involved reading and writing.

**scroll**
A roll of papyrus used for writing.

**starve**
To suffer from hunger.

**stern**
The back part of a ship.

**Tarsus**
An ancient city in modern-day Turkey, which was part of the Roman empire during Cleopatra's life.

**temples**
Buildings in which people pray and worship.

**washerwomen**
Women who wash clothes.

**wet nurse**
A woman who cares for and suckles children that are not her own.

# INDEX

# Acknowledgements

The publisher would like to thank the following for permission to reproduce their material. Every care has been taken to trace copyright holders. However, if there have been unintentional omissions or failure to trace copyright holders, we apologize and will, if informed, endeavour to make corrections in any future edition.

Key: *b* = bottom, *c* = centre, *l* = left, *r* = right, *t* = top

Pages 2 iStockphoto; 2 Corbis/Richard T Nowitz; 4*tc* Photolibrary.com; 4*bl* Art Archive/Musée du Louvre/Dagli Orti; 4*b* Photolibrary.com; 7 iStockphoto; 10 iStockphoto; 17 Getty/Stone; 21 Getty Images; 22 Bridgeman Art Library/Freud Museum, London; 23 iStockphoto/Edward E Karaa; 30 Photolibrary.com; 32 Photolibrary.com; 48 Stephane Compoint; 52 Art Archive/Musée du Louvre/Dagli Orti; 53 HIP/British Museum; 55*l* Corbis/Bettmann; 55*r* HIP/British Museum; 55*b* Art Archive/Dagli Orti; 56*l* Corbis/Bettmann; 57*t* Corbis/Wolfgang Kaehler; 57*b* Corbis/Yann Arthus-Bertrand; 58*l* Art Archive/Musée du Louvre; 58*lc* Corbis/Gianni Dagli Orti; 58*cr* Corbis/Gianni Dagli Orti; 58*r* Corbis/Gianni Dagli Orti; 58*br* Art Archive/Musée du Louvre; 59 HIP/British Museum

The publisher would like to thank Tamlyn Francis for all her help and enthusiasm.

Look out for
***Leonardo da Vinci***
by Steve Augarde
in 2008!